WOOD WORK OF GARHWAL HIMALAYA

WOOD WORK OF GARHWAL HIMALAYA

By

Dr. RICHA KAMBOJ

Assistant Professor & Head

Department of Drawing & Painting

M.K.P. (P.G.) College, Dehra Dun, Uttarakhand.

RESEARCH INDIA PRESS

New Delhi (INDIA)

ISBN : 978-93-5171-003-5

Price : ₹ 1250/-

First Edition: 2014

Published by :
RESEARCH INDIA PRESS
E-6/34, Sangam Vihar
New Delhi-110062
Phone: 011-26047013, (M) 9818085794
E-mail: researchindiapress@gmail.com

Typesetting by
G. R. Sharma

Contents

Foreword

When Dr. Richa asked me to write a foreword for her book *Woodwork of Garhwal Himalay*, the topic that has remained closest to my heart, I felt lost in the nostalgic memories of my adolescent years in the ancestral home. It was an old multi-storeyed building, in which several families lived together. We had old-fashioned sturdy and one-piece doors, with ornamental wooden bosses. The verandas had ribbed, carved and attenuated posts, with ornamental railings, balusters and the reasonably carved cusped arches between them. We also had some large wooden storage boxes, the *kothadas*, firmly jointed without nails or screws, all made of the ageless deodar wood. I do not remember if those were ever displaced from their original position. Besides, we also had some artistically made woodenwares of day-to-day use. All those things of my formative yesteryears now live in my sombre reflections only. The winds of change have swept all those artistic relics of local workmanship away. That malady is not only confined to my home; in our times, it has taken an epidemic dimension in the western Himalayan interiors, and elsewhere too.

Although, the people today are better educated, they are least conscious about the nuances of their cultural inheritance.

In fact, the consumerist psychology has rather taken grievous toll of their sense of beauty and the cultural values. The richly carved wooden temples and residential houses in the Himalayan interiors, now painted with the detesting and abrasive synthetic colours and the interiors lined and covered with the ceramic tiles, are the glaring examples of the erosion in the traditional value-system. Who would tell the people that our forefathers had better sense of conserving those edifices of popular faith and, at the same time, patronising and encouraging the art of woodcarving? The people had been occasionally applying *chulli* oil, deodar oil or linseed oil to the fragile and exposed carvings; and that way the exquisite woodcarvings lasted for centuries. If we have to protect the precious legacy of art in our temples and homes, we have to look back for the remedies in our traditional wisdom.

The type of wood-based temple or domestic architecture that has come to stay in the Garhwal Himalay or precisely in the Yamuna basin, covering the western part of Uttarakhand and eastern part of Himachal Pradesh, presents a distinctive class by itself. Although it does not differ much architecturally or functionally from its counterparts in rest of the western Himalayan region, yet the timber-bonded stone masonry walling, so popular in the Yamuna basin, is uncommon in the rest of Uttarakhand.

This vast mountainous area in the Yamuna watershed, where the wood-based architecture has been traditionally popular, is predominantly populated by the people belonging to the Khash ethnic stock. I strongly feel that the biophysical condition of this mountainous tract and the ethnic factor have been greatly responsible for the evolution of this quintessential form of wood-based architecture. Therefore, it may appropriately be defined as the Khash architecture. It forms a class by itself for its wood-based construction, immaculate nail-less joinery, multi-storeyed cantilevered construction, high-pitched curvaceous roofing, organisation of internal space, security arrangement, etc.

Notwithstanding the fact that the temple and houses built in that style are widely distributed in the mid-Himalayan belt in various geo-climatic and biophysical terrains, the vital aspects of the Khash architecture have been essentially the similar, and one may find identical architectural features occurring in the houses and temples. Thus, a Khash house or a temple in Uttarakhand, the neighbouring Himachal Pradesh or even in the Khashia village in Nepal would differ only in detail. Their broad features remain uniformly the same: the same construction material: wood, similar façade: the multi-storey trabeated elevation, identical linear layout pattern, etc.

The reason for that uniformity may not be far to seek. The Khash have originally been the highlander people of the Himalayan interiors, belonging to the wood-and-wool culture. Those ethnic traits have essentially remained intact in their traditional lifestyle. Thus, their residential houses have been wood-based, and they have remained intimately attached to their flocks of goats and sheep, following a mixed agro-pastoral routine. The ground floor or the basement of their houses is exclusively meant for the flocks. When a household has too large a flock to accommodate in the same house, a large penning enclosure, duly fenced against wild predators, is erected close by. Every house is generally equipped with an independent storage cabin, known as the *kotthar* or *kottha* in Shimla district and *tand* or *kotthadee* in Garhwal.

All aforesaid salient features notwithstanding, by far the most interesting and important aspect of the Khash architecture is the traditional structural engineering of the Khash artisans. Through centuries of usage, these hereditary artisans have perfected the technique of handling deodar wood to the optimum level of artistic and structural possibilities. These artisans possess the ingenuity and skill of building multi-storey structures entirely of wood, jointed perfectly without using metallic nail or screw. Sadly, reinforced cement concrete, tin and iron, synthetic paints, nails and screws, ceramic tiles, plywood, etc. have very effectively replaced the traditional construction material and killed the local workmanship. I do not mean that we should be infatuated with the past. Much water has flowed down the Yamuna and we also have sped very fast with the time. However, loosing our moorings with our past and the traditional knowledge system may be disastrous. Therefore, a harmonious and compatible combination of the two is the only sustainable way out.

There is a dire need to protect the precious legacy of art and culture in our temples and homes. For that, we need to retrospect for the remedies in our traditional wisdom. The synthetic materials may impart a fleeting shine our houses, but these alien formulations are certainly contraband to our wooden temples, for none of these can restore the nostalgic aurora that permeate these edifices of popular faith, rather these would inflict irreversible harm to these. Dr. Richa has very painstakingly attempted to bring out some of the vital aspects of the traditional art of woodwork that exists in the temples, but the woodwork in the residential houses of this region is equally interesting. She has lucidly expressed her concern for the survival of this important traditional art against the pernicious influence of market culture. Therefore, Dr. Richa deserves a heartily congratulation for her effort to salvage what is now left and to record that in the present volume for the benefit of posterity.

O. C. Handa

11, Shiwalik Bhawan,

Sanjauli, Shimla-171006

Preface

Socio-culturally the Garhwal Himalayas, once the seat of Kulindas in ancient past, constituted a rich belt of the new state of Uttarakhand. Though it attracted the attention of sociologist in the twentieth century for its old typical polyandrous social order, the indigenous art of wood carving scattered in the deep interiors, particularly the wooden components of the local temples of the natives situated in the villages, virtually remained neglected for any comprehensive study until the author took its survey for the research in the beginning of the present century.

Though, historically, the art of wood carving is known to be very old in India as suggested by its imitations in the architectural components witnessed in the rock-art caves of Bhaja, it seems to be a natural outcome of the socio geographical features in the vast expense of the whole Himalayan region where wood was the staple raw material easily available in the forests surrounding the habitats of the natives. In due course of time, wood acquired both the functional as well as the aesthetic significance in their lives. Instinctively, out of awe and adoration, man decorated the places of worship. This resulted in the rich tradition of wood carving in the temples of the natives of the Himalayan belt where wood was employed as the major component of the architecture.

The thrust areas of the present study are the two major regions of the Garhwal Himalayas- the Jaunsar- Bawar and Rawain, where the religious edifices were often dedicated to the local deities or legendary heroes of the great epics. These two regions yield the most outstanding, prominent and quintessential examples of wood-work in the Garhwal Himalaya. Waves of socio-political and socio-religious events of the past left their traces on the local beliefs and practices. During extensive survey of these regions the author discovered that the themes related to Brahamanical sources were quite popular and found frequent visual manifestation in the wood carvings of the religious edifices situated invariably in the remote villages of this region, which have been dealt from different perspective, in detail, in the present book.

The local artisans have their own approach to their interpretations of the virtues of the motifs and deities as conditioned by their socio-cultural background, local folk-lore as well as skill, which in my opinion has bestowed their art an indigenous original flavor. What has been importantly realized in my study spread over more than a decade, is that limitation of skill sometimes results in most imaginative and creative expression.

But unfortunately, the recent encroachment of modernity and lack of serious attempt to preserve our ancient and indigenous traditional heritage, is resulting in fast degradation of the specimen of our heritage under the wake of renovation of these monuments.

The present volume is a humble attempt to record the result of my survey, documentation and critical appraisal of the dying art of native wood carving of this region – the Garhwal Himalaya, for the scholars and the posterity.

Richa Kamboj

Acknowledgements

I extend my very sincere gratitude to Dr. O.C. Handa, who has greatly contributed to the art, culture and history of the Himalayan region with many publications to his credit, whose able guidance and expertise helped me to accomplish my work successfully. I extend my sincere thanks and gratitude to my father, Prof. (Retd) B.P. Kamboj, who had been a great support to me during my visit to all the sites and centres, most of which were located in remote interior. He has been deeply associated with the hilly areas all through his life and has to his credit significant publications on the art of the hill state of Uttarakhand. His able guidance and advice and thorough discussions with him on the subject had been very relevant while accomplishing the present task. I am thankful to Dr. Madhu Jain, Head, Dept. of Drawing and Painting, Munna Lal Khemka (P.G) College, Saharanpur, whose guidance and help has always been available to me, as and when it was required.

I also express my sincere thanks to Shri Virendra Bangroo, Documentation Officer, Visual Unit, Indira Gandhi National Centre for Arts, New Delhi, who helped me immensely by making available to me valuable source material (books, journals and research papers etc.) and for extending valuable advice to me from time to time.

I also express thanks to Library In-charge and other members of the library staff of MKP (PG) College, Dehradun, for their full cooperation and prompt help extended to me. I am also thankful to the Head Librarian and the staff of the Library of Indira Gandhi National Centre for Arts, New Delhi for their cooperation and allowing me access to necessary information required during the present endeavour.

I extend my very sincere thanks to the Principal, M.K.P.(P.G.) College, whose co-operation and support helped me to complete the present work successfully.

Last but not the least, I extend very sincere thanks to my family, especially my mother Smt. Indira Kamboj and daughter Kaushiki Kamboj, whose support helped me to accomplishing the present task.

Dr. Richa Kamboj
Head Dept. of Drawing & Painting
MKP (PG) College, Dehradun.

List of Plates

Coloured Plates

Line Drawings

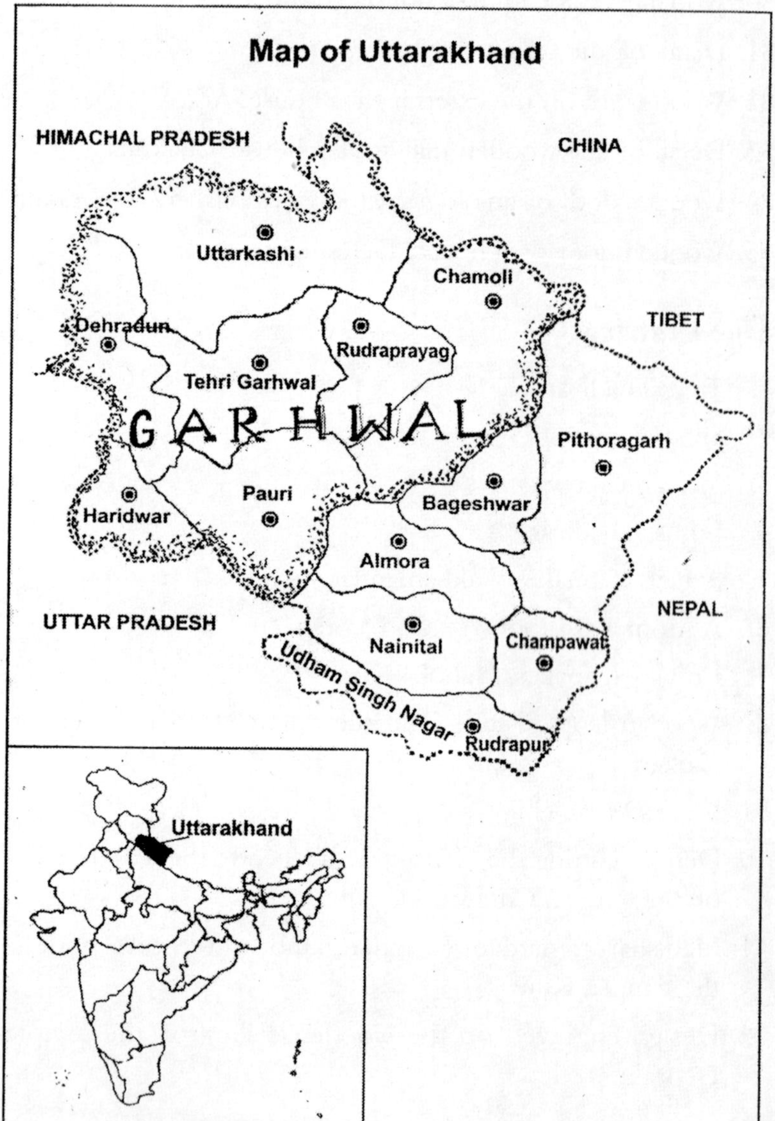

Map of Uttarakhand.

1

Introduction

GEOGRAPHICAL SETTING

The Post Independence period in India, initially resulted into formation of four districts in the hill region of United Provinces, namely – Almora, Nainital, Pauri and Dehradun. Subsequently, the district of Tehri Garhwal was formed in 1948. Uttarakhand *mandal* with three districts was formed in 1960. These newly created districts were – Uttarkashi, Chamoli and Pithoragarh. "Uttarakashi district was constituted by combining the Parganas of Rawain and Uttarkashi of the Rawain *tehsil* of Tehri Garhwal district."[1] Rawain *pargana* formed a part of Tehri state in the British period. The Uttarakhand *mandal* was abolished in December 1968 and in its place two *mandals*, namely – Kumaon and Garhwal were created. The districts of Uttarkashi, Chamoli, Tehri Garhwal, Pauri Garhwal and Dehradun came under Garhwal *mandal*. The districts of Pithoragarh, Almora and Nainital constituted the Kumaon *mandal*.

The state of Uttaranchal came into existence in 2000. The hill region of Uttar Pradesh included nine districts (Hardwar being the ninth besides eight mentioned above). The newly created state included thirteen districts now. The three districts which came into existence were Rudraprayag,Champawat and Udham Singh Nagar. Later the name of the state was changed from Uttaranchal to Uttrarakhand.

The districts of the new state of Uttrarakhand were sub-divided into *tehsil* and *parganas*. Thus the *tehsils* of the British period which included a larger area were further sub-divided into smaller areas forming *parganas.*

The two prominent centres of wood work in Garhwal Himalaya are- Jaunsar-Bawar and Rawain regions. Inspire of all these subdivisions implemented after the creation of the new state of Uttarakhand, Jaunsar–Bawar and Rawain regions are known and recognized in their old wider geographical context when the socio-cultural heritage of these regions is discussed. Though the political sub-divisions caused these *parganas* of Jaunsar–Bawar and Rawain Tehsil to lose their old physical boundaries of the British period, yet they still retain the old identity so far as their affinity in respected of the socio-religious and socio-cultural heritage is concerned.

Jaunsar–Bawar region lies to the north of Dehra Dun tehsil and constitutes a part of Dehradun district of Uttarakhand state. It covers an area of 342.5 square miles and is situated between north latitude 30°-31' and 31°–3'–30" east longitude 77°-45' and 78° – 7'–20."[2] It is bounded in the east by Tehri Garhwal, on the west by Himachal Pradesh and on the south by Dehradun *tehsil.* This region constitutes of two major sub divisions, namely – Jaunsar and Bawar. According to Atkinson Jaunsar-Bawar *pargana* in fact contains a third, known locally as Lokhandi.[3] Jaunsar is bounded on the east by the Yamuna and by the Tons on the west with their junction at Kalsi with a total length of eighteen miles from north to south. It is followed by Lohkandi in the north with a length of five miles. To the north of Lohkandi is Bawar with a length of ten miles. Its total length from north to south is 33 miles and its breadth being 23 miles at the widest.[4]

The major portion of the entire region of Jaunsar – Bawar and Rawain falls in the Lesser Himalaya range with the exception of northern-most area of Rawain which falls in the Greater Himalayan zone. The river Yamuna which flows along the eastern edge of Jaunsar–Bawar *pargana*, rises from the Yamnotri Glacier. The river Tons situated in the western portion of Jaunsar–Bawar *pargana*, is the major tributary of Yamuna, originating from the Bandarpunch glacier.

Jaunsar-Bawar is basically hilly and mountainous region. The typical physical feature of the region is a ridge which originates at Haripuar Byas near Kalsi and runs west of Chakrata, Deoban and then in a north-easterly direction to the Kharamba peak above Lokar. At Bairat, there is a peak having an elevation of 7,399 feet above the sea level. Another peak at Kyawa has an elevation of 6,558 feet. Deoban is 9,331 feet, Bajamari 9,536 feet and three other peaks, 9,200, 9,533 and 10,075 feet respectively. The ridge then enters Tehri and loses itself in the spurs of Bandarpunch.[5]

The Jaunsar-Bawar region is rich in forest area having variety of trees like oak, spruce fir, deodar, pine etc. The area near *Kalsi* has *sal, bakli, dhoora, haldu, kusam, khair* and *sisu*. Between an altitude of 5,000 to 7,500 feet grey oak, rhododenaron and andromeda are found. At the lower limit the chir pine and at the upper, blue pine and the *deodar*, and above these, *deodar*, *moru* and *karshu* oaks. Besides maple, horse chestnut, walnut, cypress, spruce, silver fir, yew and pyrus are also found in this region.[6] The most significant of forests of the region consists of vigorous vegetation of *deodar*.

Rawain region, a main centre of wood work in Garhwal Himalaya, falls west of the Alaknanda river up to the north-western and south western boundaries of the state or of District Uttarkashi. It formed a part of the Rawain *tehsil* in Tehri Garhwal district in 1948 and of the Tehri state in the British period. Rawain *tehsil* constituted of two *parganas* – Rawain and Uttarkashi.

During the British period Rawain *pargana* was situated to the east of the Jaunsar–Bawar *pargana*, with its western extent stretching up to the river Alaknanda. Walton, in his Gazetteer of Garhwal Himalaya, mentions that, "Mr. Fraser in 1815 was authorized to hand over to Raja Sudarshan Shah, the portion of Garhwal situated to the west of the Alakanda with the express reservation of the Dun and the *pargana* Rawain lying between the Alaknanda and the Bhagirathi……. It was subsequently suggested by Mr. Gardber that Rawain, the barren and rocky country between Nagpur and Jaunsar-Bawar, containing the headquarters of the Tons, the Jumuna and the Bhagirathi, be handed over to the Raja of Garhwal ……."[7]

Thus the extent of Rawain region considered for the purpose of our study includes the area which lies to the west of the river Alaknanda rising from Vishnuprayag and flowing south-west up to Nandprayag where it receives Mandakini and further reaches Karn- parayag where it receives the river Pindar. Here it turns westward and at Rudraprayag it receives the river Mandakini. It flows south-ward and at Deoprayag it is joined by Bhagirathi where onwards it is known as the Ganga. The Bhagirathi originates near Gaumukh from the Gangotri glacier. River Bhilangana, a tributary of Bhagirathi, originates in the Kedarnath glacier zone and its confluence with the Bhagirathi river occurs at Tehri.

The river Tons originates from the southern base of the same mountains from which the Yamuna takes its origin but at a distance of a few miles. It flows in western direction for about thirty miles till its confluence occurs with Rupin situated to the north of the former. The Tons, from its source to its confluence with Rupin, is also known as the Supin, but after confluence it becomes Tons. After flowing for about nineteen miles it receives the Pabar and after further thirteen miles it receives the Shaboi. The Tons flows in the southern direction demarcating the Jaunsar–Bawar region from the state of Himachal Pradesh. After a total course of about 100 miles its confluence with Yamuna occurs at Kalsi at an altitude of 1636 feet (situated at latitude 30°-30' and longitude 77°-52)[8]

SOCIO-RELIGIOUS BACKGROUND OF THE REGION

Garhwal Himalaya projects panoramic view of the social life of indigenous people, nurtured with cultural prosperity, artistic pursuits in different genres whether it is miniature painting or wood work and the religious view of this belt is coloured with a rainbow of local cults as well as Brahmanical followings. The outstanding centres of wood work of this belt- Jaunsar-Bawar and Rawain regions are also rich so far their socio-religio and religio-cultural aspects are concerned. The inhabitants of Jaunsar–Bawar are referred to as Jaunsaris and those of Rawain are known as Rawantas. The former have been declared scheduled tribes by the Government of India in 1967. The inhabitants of Rawain are also "almost tribal in their life style but they have not been included in the list of scheduled tribes by the government."[9]

According to Walton the rural population of Garhwal comprises of Biths & Doms. Two major castes constitute the Biths are further subdivided into Brahmans and Khas-Brahamans, and Rajputs and Khas-Rajputs.[10]

Khasas

The Khasas are believed to have hailed from Central Asia at an early time. Reference to Khasas is frequently found in Sanskrit literature. The latter contains frequent references to a tribe whose name is invariably spelt Khasa, with variants such as Khosa, Khasa and Khasira.[11]

According to Walton, "the Khas-Rajputs are the Khasiyas, whose claim to be immigrants from an Aryan source are generally allowed."[12] They initially inhabited the extreme north west of India, the Hindu Kush and the mountainous tracts to the south as well as the western Punjab.[13] They were looked down upon by the Aryans who called them Bhartya or Malaichha since they did not observe the rules and practices related to eating and drinking followed by Aryans. Later their position was improved when they came to be considered the off springs of *Kshatriyas* of *Vratya* caste as mentioned in *Manusmriti*.[14] The Khasas were a war-like tribe. They were physically strong and powerful people. It was probably this quality which won them the name Khasa, since Khasiya or Khashiya in Garhwal has similar cannotations.[15]

The Khasas find mention in *Mahabharata*. They were in the army of Duryodhan against Pandavs in the battle of Kurukshetra. Armed with swords and lances they fought with stones against Satyaki, "Fighting with stones was well-known in the hills.[16] Duryodhan is worshipped in Jaunsar region. A temple dedicated to Duryodhan is situated at Saur. Thus there seems to be affinities between the present day Khasa inhabitants with the ancient Khasas of Mahabharat times. The Jaunsaris worship Duryodhan as god Somesu. The Pandavs are worshipped in the other parts of Garhwal. The physiognomy of Khasas is characterized by long bearded face, long and straight nose, abundant moustaches, slightly fair to wheatish complexion, tall and burly body, hazel eyes and curly hair. The Khasiya sub castes are the Negis, Bishts and Rawats.[17]

Doms

The Doms are aboriginal inhabitants of the region. They were treated as surfs by the Khasas. Their four sub-classes in Garhwal are the *Kolis*, *Tamolas* or *Tamta*, *Lohars* and Ors. The Doms are low caste people who include the blacksmiths, carpenters, weavers, musicians, shoemakers etc. R.D. Mazumdar believes that Doms have a higher racial status than generally ascribed to them. "It is possible that both the Doms and the Chamars have had a higher cultural status and their present low social position and general degradation was due to social or political disabilities imposed on them from outside.[18]

Rawantlas

"The inhabitants of Rawain of Uttarkashi district are called Rawantlas. Rawanatlas are geographically in Garhwal region but they are quite different from Garhwalis in their social and cultural set up. Anthropogenically also they are more akin to Jaunsaris and the people of Sirmaur (a border district of Himachal Pradesh). Thus they may be associated with much discussed Khasa people on the ground of physical, cultural, social and religious similarities,"[19]

The caste structure of Rawain region enfolds the Brahmins, the Rajputs, the Naths, the Bajgis, the Mistris the Lohars, the Koltas, the Doms and the Chamars. The three classes of castes which are described in the region are: the upper caste which includes the Brahmins and the Rajputs, the middle caste which includes the Naths, the Bajgis, the Mistris and the Lohars. The middle caste includes basically the artisans. The lower castes include the Koltas, the Doms and the

Chamars.[20] The Brahmins conduct rituals and perform the role of priest. Naitwar is an exception where a Rajput performs the role of a priest. The Bajgis clear utensils in the marriage of the Brahmins and the Rajputs. Besides they are also temple cleaner and also beat the drum at dawn, noon, dusk and night in a temple since they also work as the attendant to temple priest. The Naths are the fallout of the Shavite *panth* which once dominated the area. They are custodians of the temple lore. [21] The Koltas are agricultural workers and the Doms perform all menial jobs and dispose the dead animals. They are skinners, curriers and tanners.

Polyandry was in practice in both Jaunsar-Bawar and Rawain regions. With the rise of literacy rate, education level and employment of the inhabitants in good jobs, the practice of polyandry is gradually decreasing in the area.

The status of women had been low in the region. The marriage system included bride price or marriage by sale, levirate marriage of widows and divorcees.

The region has a rich repertoire of the folk tradition – folk songs, folklore, folk dance and folk art. A number of festivals are celebrated here on different occasions adding gay, different hues and colours to the life of the people. *Bissu* is a festival and fair which is celebrated in each and every village in Rawain and Jaunsar–Bawar. *Selku* and *Laang* are sport festivals celebrated with much fervor. *Devlang* is another sport festival celebrated in Rawain region in which trial of strength takes place between the devotees (a symbolic remnant of the old rivalry between the Kauravs and the Pandavs). Thus fairs and sport festivals infuse the people of the region with a new and tremendous energy to help them confront and tackle the adverse and challenging circumstances imposed by the remote and difficult mountainous habitats they dwell in.

The popular folk arts, folk plays and folk dances hold great significance in the community life of these people and need our special attention, Pandav dance or *lila* is much in practice in the remote areas of Uttarkashi district. They reflect religio-social life and beliefs of the aboriginals.

References

1. Handa, O. C. History of Uttaranchal (Indus Publishing Company, New Delhi, 2002) P. 212.
2. Atkinson, E.T. The Himalayan Gazetteer Vol. 3 Part I., (Low Price Publication, Delhi) p. 339.
3. *Ibid.*
4. *Ibid*, p. 340.
5. *Ibid*, p. 341.
6. *Ibid*, p. 342.
7. Walton, H.G. Gazetteer of *Garhwal Himalaya* (Natraj Publishers, Dehradun, 1989) p. 130.
8. Atkinson, *Op.Cit.*, Vol. 3, part-II, p. 714.
9. Saklani, D.P. 'Tribal Populace : Distribution, Lifestyle, Tradition and Change', in, Garhwal Himalaya, Nature, Culture & Society, edited by Kandari & Gusain (Trans Media, Media House, Srinagar, Garhwal, 2001) p. 360.
10. Walton, *Op.Cit.* p. 60.
11. Saklani, *Op.Cit.* p. 357 (His source is Grierson, G.A., Linguisitc Survey of India, Government Press, Calcutta, Vol. IX, 1916).
12. Walton, *Op.Cit.* p. 60.
13. Saklani, *Op.Cit.* p. 357.
14. Handa, O.C. *Paschimi Hiamalay Ki Lok Kalayen* (Indus Publishing Company, New Delhi, 1988), p. 21.
15. Nautiyal, Shivananda, *Garhwal Ka Sanskritik Vaibhav* (Uttar Madhya Kendra, Sanskritik Kendra, Allahabad, 1994) p. 9.

16. Saklani, *Op. Cit.* p. 358.
17. Walton, *Op.Cit.* p. 62.
18. Mazumdar, D.N. Races and Cultures of India (Universal Publishers Ltd., Lucknow, 1944) p. 37.
19. Saklani, *Op.Cit.* pp. 359-360.
20. Bhatt, G.S. Women and Polyandry in Rawain Jaunpur (Rawat Publication, Jaipur, 1991) p. 23.
21. *Ibid.* p. 25.

2

Wood Carving

WOOD CARVING IN HISTORICAL PERSPECTIVE

In ancient times, when the nation was blessed with less population and more of open fields, hills and *tarai* regions of the country were covered with dense forests, wood was an easily available material for the construction of structural components of the buildings. It was employed in the construction of doors, door-jambs, balconies and brackets and also roof and floors were made of wood.

Nature has bestowed man with innate aesthetic instincts which ever since the Neolithic period in particular, found expression in beautification and embellishment of his own-self as well as in creation of objects of daily use, giving them elegant shapes and decorating these with exquisite geometrical and naturalistic motifs. Huge wealth of the objects made of stone, bones, clay, metal and wood of this period found everywhere in the world are testimony to this belief and its universality. Over the ages, a rich tradition of creative arts and crafts developed everywhere, evolving into distinct regional styles. Wood having being associated with one of man's basic needs – the shelter, and also being easier material to deal with, to chisel and carve than stone, became a popular medium for the primitive craftsmen to display their creative skill. Thus, the architectural activities in the Garhwal Himalaya were initially largely executed in wood, as it was not solely easily available construction material but from the point of view of the climatic conditions of the region, it definitely suited more since the wooden edifices remain warm and cozy in cold weather in comparison to those using stone and concrete. The latter remain cold and are unsuitable for the cold weather condition of this belt which is also earth quake prone. The architectural components of these wooden edifices were embellished with variety of decorative and symbolic motifs, scenes derived from mythological sources, socio-religious life and popular beliefs. This resulted in a vast and rich repertoire of beautifully carved wooden motifs of great variety– floral, geometrical, religio-mythological, secular and social, exhibiting local and native styles and identity. These specimens served not only the decorative purpose but also became the representative of the rare artifacts preserving the peculiar characteristics of the culture of particular social and regional group (races, tribes, castes etc.). Traces of the ancient tradition of wood- carving and its use as an architectural component can be witnessed in their imitation in the rock-cut caves of Bhaja.

Primarily, originating from such primordial roots, with transition from the primitive through rural to the urban developments, some of these arts and crafts, not only persisted but rose to the eminence for their peculiar merits to national and international fame. In India in particular, from Kashmir to the southern peninsula, various centres are today known for wood carving for centuries.

Ever since the Neolithic period, mankind has cherished an innate desire to adorn his body and the objects of utility in life. The inborn aesthetic sense with which man was blessed, spiritual and mundane needs, socio-environmental factors of Garhwal Himalaya led to a rich tradition of the practice of intricate carving on the structural components of the edifices erected in the region. Regarding the antiquity of use of wood, for architecture and scripture, O.P. Agarwal renders useful information, "In ancient India wood was the most popular medium for making sculptures and carving and for architecture. In fact, architecture and sculpture have always been intimately connected with each other and the study of one, therefore, is related to the study of the other. Ample mention of the art of wood carving is found in the early literature of India. It is mentioned in the *Vedas* (1500 B.C.- 800 B.C) and also in the great epics Mahabharata and Ramayana (C. 1000 B.c.). The palaces of Chandragupta Maurya (4th cent B.C.) at Pataliputra were made of wood. That timber was extensively used for the construction of buildings and, therefore, for carving purposes during the Mauryan period is shown by Magasthenes' account of the Mauryain capital of Pataliputra (near Patna). This Greek Ambassador resided at the court of the Emperor Chandragupta. According to his description, timber was the most popular building material. That gold and silver were used for ornamentation of wood work becomes apparent from his depiction of the Royal Palaces in which the pillars of wood were entwined by vines embossed in gold and ornamented with designs of birds and foliage in gold and silver [1].......The use of wood in India for carving purposes from very early times has been reported in many scholarly writings [2, 3, 4]. The great importance that was attached to the use of wood for architecture and image-making in ancient times becomes apparent in the description of the careful selection of wood for these purposes by contemporary Indian texts on architecture and iconography. The *Vishnudharmottara*, a text of the 6th century A.D., mentions in great details the use and selection of wood for architecture [5]. The *Brihad Samhita* of *Varah Mihira*, datable to the 7th century A.D. [6], also gives detailed instructions on the use of wood. Easy availability of timber and comparative ease of working it either in relief or in the round was one of the main reasons for its abundant use for artistic expression. In India image worship is of great antiquity, and this practice must have resulted in the production of many idols."[1]

Indecently, the city close to Uttarakhand, and famous for its wood-carving crafts, is Saharanpur (also a district of Uttar Pradesh bordering the southern part of Uttarakhand). Today it can boast of international recognition for its wood work and the great variety of its products with beautifully carved intricate designs and shapes.

It is flanked by the Ganga in the east and the Yamuna in the west with the vast Shivalik range separating it from Uttarakhand to its north. It enjoyed a congenial location for the flourishing woodcraft serving both the aesthetic and utilitarian needs. The craftsmen here are known for their skills in handicrafts as well as for the wooden structural components of buildings. The main raw-material required for these the craft is *sisham* or *sal* wood which has been available in abundance in the forests of the *tarai* region and the Shivalik range adjoining the city of Saharanpur. The history of art bears testimony to the fact that the easy availability of raw material has always served as a favorable factor for the growth and development of the craft at a place and shaping of the religio- aesthetic and socio-cultural character of the respective particular place and the people.

Though no concrete evidence of artistic activity in wood craft has so far so been discovered belonging to the ancient times so far, yet the hypothesis that wood was employed for construction of the houses and/or their structural components, has been in vogue in the ancient times cannot be ruled out. "Paradoxically enough, the decorative architecture developed in India out of wood. Stone overtook it during the classical age. In the medieval times we find the history repeating itself when the lithic decorative devices of the classical architecture are being replicated in wood.[2]

In India, the art of wood carving is believed to have been introduced through Persia for the first time in Kashmir. The Persian craftsmen migrated from their country due to shortage of the *shisham* wood which got exhausted due to its use for manufacturing charcoal. The immigrant craftsmen from Persia to Kashmir proved their proficiency of wood carving in the walnut wood. The socio-economic instability due to the disturbance of tranquility of Kashmir in 1817 resulting in the fall of Mughal rule in Kashmir, caused the wood craftsmen to migrate to Multan in the undivided Punjab (now in Pakistan), Saharanpur and some other places in the then United Provinces of Agra and Oudh (now part of Uttar Pradesh), e.g. Nagina, (Bijnor district). Aligarh, Azamgarh, Bareilly, Badayun, Bulandshahr, Mainpuri, Farrukhabad, etc. Some wood carvers are even believed to have moved directly from Iran to Saharanpur as they were not adept in handling walnut wood whereas *shisham* wood was found in exuberance in the *doab* and *dun* forests.[3]

The city of Saharanpur has yielded some examples of fine and quintessential wood carving on the structural components of the buildings belonging to the early medieval period. The ancient period must have also witnessed artistic activity on wooden components of the *havelis* of the region, the sufficient examples of which have been found which, "provide us with valuable clues of the past times and enable us to establish a continuity of the classical art tradition of the past Gurjar-Pratihara age in the Ganga-Jamuna doab area to the recent past."[4]

After the advent of the wood craftsmen from Kashmir to Saharanpur in 1817, the prior indigenous style of religio-aesthetic wood work on the structural components of the buildings paved way to amalgamation of Indo-Persian decorative motifs and technique associated with the wood craft. The indigenous element of the earlier period includes the carving of the *lata-pallava* and similar other motifs. During the Muslim region in Indo-Gangetic plains, the impact of Islamic art executed its influence on the religio-aesthetic motifs executed on the wooden components of the old buildings, and it received further aggravation due to migration of wood–carvers of Kashmir to Saharanpur and other cities. The lattice work, i.e. the fret-saw perforation, so popular at Saharanpur, is of Persian origin and is known as *pinjara*.

Another famous centre of wood–carving handicaft is Nagina in the district of Bijnor. Here the specimens of wood crafts are found in the form of different articles like picture frames, chairs, tables, caskets, walking stickes, all often richly embellished with floral and ornamental motifs.

It was during the British period, that, when the Britishers introduced the wooden articles produced at Saharanpur in England and their demand increased greatly due to admiration they received there, that subsequently wood-based art activity took the form of a small scale industry here.

SIGNIFICANCE OF WOOD-CARVINGS IN GARHWAL HIMALAYA

Wood is the staple raw material found in exuberance in the forests providing a shield to the entire vast expansion of the

Himalayan range lying to the north and north-east of the country. Its easy availability served as the major factor resulting in its employment in the construction of residential as well as religious architecture of the entire region which apart from its functional purpose, also quenched the aesthetic thirst of the dwellers and commissioners, i.e. the local inhabitants of the villages as well as that of the artisans entrusted with the task. The initial building activity of the hilly areas of the country in the ancient times had been largely, or rather it will not be exaggeration to claim, was solely dependent on wood as the main raw-material.

Though, due to the perishable character of wood very old specimens of wooden structures did not survive in the hilly region. Yet, "one can get a glimpse of excellence of wooden architecture of Kashmir from the 8th century painted wooden frame of a shrine enshrining Buddha made of ivory, ….. The wooden frame is the miniature composition of a temple having architectural elements of the double pyramidal roof in combination with three-foil niches and pillars."[5] It is in the collection of Gopikrishna Kanaria, Patna. Similar architecture frames made of *deodar* wood, one enshrining Siddhartha with attending *chaur*i-bearers, is in the Cleveland Museum of Art and another is in the British Museum, London.[6]

Besides, easy availability of the wood, the hilly regions receiving heavy rainfall and snowfall, wood was a congenial building material. Besides the buildings constructed of wood retain warmth and coziness for considerable longer period of time than buildings constructed with stones and bricks. Moreover, hilly regions being prone to earth-quakes, interlocked wooden beams used in the walls were more resistant and durable to endure any such calamity. Thus whether it was rich or poor, in ancient times, wood was a stable building material for the both. Those who belonged to the wealthy class, for the pacification of their aesthetic urge and socio-religio faiths, they got their houses carved with motifs of relilgio-aesthetic significance. It was an important factor in the origin and development of the art of wood carving in the regions concerned. Besides, so far as the religious architecture is concerned, carving of symbolic and geometric motifs and religious themes were deemed necessary to propagandize the faith among the followers, specially the illiterate class. Contents of the religious and mythological themes contained in the religious scriptures and carving of the auspicious symbolic motifs added an aura of divinity and purity to the religious architecture. Thus the art of wood carving flourished in the Himalayan region and the techno-aesthetic aspects associated with it also achieved perfection in due course of time.

Among the trees which provide timber for temple construction, *deodar* is very important, since, it is esteemed as very auspicious, pure and sacred. It is believed to be naturally vested with divine qualities, perhaps especially due to its insecticidal character which lends it great durability. According to H.G. Walton, "It is known that in the earlier days of the British occupation the country on either side of the main ridge was thickly covered with noble forests of deodar, and it is along it and its spurs that existing forests occur. …… The deobar range derives its name from the double peak (9,331 feet) which towers above Chakrata. The immediate vicinity of the mountain now contain but little deodar for which it was once noted, but a few scattered plantations have been formed. ……. But the glory of Jaunsar- Bawar is its virgin forests of deodar. …………"[7] The Bodhyar, Mashak and Kotikanesar forests are found on the Lokhandi spur, the Konain forests on the spur between the Binal and Shili streams, the Tutwa Maura and

Lakhan forests are located around the head of the Dharagadh. Towards the west of the latter the Kathian, Koti and Panch Koti forests are found. The Murach forest are to the west of the Tons. All through the ridges, large forests of oak, fir, spruce and scattered patches of *deodar* are found. South of Kalsi *sal* and other subordinate species are found.[8]

Vast expanse of deodar forests are found along the western Dhauli between Kark and Malari in the Niti Valley and near Pandukeswar and around the Binsar temple. "The large number of deodar sleepers has been exported from Pandukeshwar."[9]

This divine wood, deodar, is also known by several other names in different classical Sanskrit texts, i.e., *daru, surahiv, suradrum, suradaru, daruka surapadap, devahv, devadrum, devakashtth, devahvay, Mahadary, amaradary, amarakashtth* etc.[10] The latter two names of *deodar*, *amara* + *daru* and *amara* + *kashtth,* as the names suggest and define this wood as possessing immortal quality or the quality of surviving for posterity. "According to the folk belief, the deodar wood will last for at least one thousand years in water; it may last for five to ten times more in air."[11] It is due to all these divine virtues associated with deodar wood that, for the construction of temple architecture, it was exclusively employed in the Himalaya regions of the country. Use of wood in the construction of the ceiling etc. is also seen in the mosque in Kashmir. "The distinctive form of wooden architecture can be noticed in the mosque of Madin Sahib Zadibal….. The ceiling is made up of thin pieces of wood worked into geometrical patterns and supported on four wooden columns."[12] The mosque has a pyramidal roof. Thus the architectural activities in the hilly regions of all the religions in the ancient times, were to a considerable extent wood based.

Uttarakhand had a tradition of worshiping tree deities even at an earlier date in about the fourth and fifth century B.C.

Wooden statues or rocks were kept beside three trunk and were worshipped. No wooden temple dating to ancient period has been discovered from Uttarakhand due to the perishable quality of wood and religio-political factors. Changes must have also caused the ancient wooden temples to perish. Walton renders us with significant information regarding Yamnotri, "The temple in Tehri state, situated in 31° 1'N, and 78'28 E. It stands on the western flanks of the great peak of Bandarpunch (20°, 73' at an elevation of about 10,800 feet above the sea and 4 miles below the glacier from which the Jamuna issues. The temple is a small wooden structure and contains an image of the goddess Jumuna."[13] The wooden temple at Yamnotri was built by Sudarshan Shah after 1850 A.D. It was later replaced by a stone temple built by Pratap Shah.[14]

The present temple at Gangotri was built by King Madho Singh of Jaipur in early 20th Cen. A.D. Fraser mentions that there was no temple at Gangotri in the beginning of the 19th century A.D.. According to Shiv Prasad Naithani, the monastery at Gangotri was in ruinous state in 1788 A.D. and he further believes that the monastery or temple, at this date which was probably a wooden temple.[15] Thus, it can be assumed on the basis of the evidences and references found so far, that wool served as a primary medium for all the architectural activities all through the Himalayan belt of the country. "At the sites where we find stone temples of *nagar* style now, there is great possibility in ancient times wooden temples existed."[16] The wooden doors of the sun temple of Katarmal in Kumaon, render significant evidence about existence of wooden temples earlier to medieval period in Uttarakhand. "The recovery of a 5.10 ft. wooden pillar of nine-tenth century CE with *mangalaghats,* encircled with *Nagas* and standing divine images in the middle from Katarmal, preserved in the National

Museum, New Delhi, indicate that before the construction of the present temple there existed a wooden temple which was replaced somewhere in the thirteenth-fourteenth century CE by a Katyuri ruler"[17].

Besides, residential structures in this region initially must have also relied on wood only as primary raw material. Necessity of bigger religious and residential buildings resulting in expansion of the space of the exteriors and additional rooms serving different utility objectives. The architectural device employed to achieve this end involved a combination of stone and wood in the walls. But wood is the principal architectural component which provides great structural strength to the edifice as a binding factor. "The whole structure rests on a frame of thick wooden beams of deodars rectangular or square, each interlocked with the other. Two to four rows of chiseled stones are laid over them followed by another frame of deodar beams. This is repeated upto the desired height. The sturdy wooden frames for the doors, windows or ventilators are provided and they too are interlocked with the wooden beams, which at the base and the top, extend further to support the wooden structure of the floor of the verandah or *mandap* or balcony and the gable or pent roof above.[18] This technique of dove-tailing wooden beams at corners provides earthquake resistance to the edifice. Such wall types are known as *katth-kuni*. The wooden framework is known as the *cheolchzatairi*, or patari in the vernacular parlance. The course of dry stone is locally called *maid*, and "similar type of wall, having a number of dry stone courses between the *cheols*, is known as *dhol-maide*" [19]

Sometimes use of wood is further minimized by using wooden planks instead of scantlings and joints. This technique of wall construction, known as *farque*, was probably introduced in Chamba (H.P.) through Kashmir, can be noticed near Naitwar in the interiors of Uttarkashi district of Uttarakhkand and also in the walls of residential houses in the eastern districts of Uttarakhand.[20]

Thus wood plays a significant role in the entire hilly regions of the country. *Deodar* commands great reverence and it is chiefly employed in the construction and renovation of the temple architecture. The household wooden wares are usually made of some local varieties of wood, especially in the eastern part of Uttarakhand. Local wood, known as *sanad* and *getthi* are used to make such objects.[21] Easy availability of wood, its eco-friendly features, suitability to the cold climate of the hilly regions, proficiency of the indigenous artisans in carving wood are some of the factors which are responsible for the significance of wood in religious as well as secular edifices in the hilly regions and they also led to the popularity of wood based handicrafts and its use in household utensils.

References

1. Agarwal, O.P. 'A Study of Indian Polychrome Wooden Sculpture', in, *Studies in Conservation*, Vol. 16, No.2, (May 1971), pp. 56-68.
2. Handa, O.C., & Jain, Madhu, *Wood Handicraft : A Study of Its Origin and Development in Saharanpur* (Indus Publishing Company, New Delhi, 2000), p. 36.
3. *Ibid.*, pp. 43,44.
4. *Ibid*, p. 36.
5. Bangroo, Virendra, 'Indigenous Architectural Heritage of Kashmir', in; Heritage of Jammu Kashmir and Ladakh. Ed., G.L. Badam, K.K. Chakravarty (Research India Press, New Delhi, 2010), p.81.
6. *Ibid.*
7. Walton, H.G. Gazetteer of Dehradun (Natraj Publishers, Dehradun, 1995), p. 21.
8. *Ibid.*

9. Walton, H.G. British Garhwal; A Gazetteer, Vol. XXXVI of the *District Gazetteers of the United Provinces of Agra and Oudh.* (Natraj Publishers, Dehradun, 1989), p. 21.

10. Handa, O.C. Woodcarving in the Himalayan Region (Indus Publishing Company, New Delhi and Institute of Integrated Himalayan Studies, HP Univ., Shimla, 2006) p. 17.

11. *Ibid*, p. 25, His source is Bernier, M. Ronald, Himalayan Towers-Temples and Palaces of Himachal Pradesh, New Delhi, 1989, p.9

12. Bangroo, *Op.Cit.*, p. 82.

13. Walton, *Op.Cit*, (1989), p. 215.

14. Naithani, Shiv Prasad, Uttarakhand ke Tirtha Evam Mandir (Parvatiya Prakashan, Srinagar, Garhwal, 1997), p. 106.

15. *Ibid*, pp. 136-137, 139.

16. Kamboj, Richa, Wooden Temples of Uttarakhand : A study of Art and Architecture (Indus Publishing Company, New Delhi,2010), p. 68.

17. Sharma, D.D. *Cultural History of Uttarkhand* (Indira Gandhi National Centre for the Arts, New Delhi, 2009), p.307

18. *Ibid*, p. 69.

19. Handa, *Op.Cit*, (2006), p. 27.

20. *Ibid*, p. 28.

21. *Ibid*, p. 129.

3

The Main Centres of Wood Carving in Garhwal Himalaya

JAUNSAR-BAWAR

Wood carving in the Garhwal Himalaya forms a part of the secular and religious architecture, mainly spread over the vast expanse of its two most significant - Jaunsar-Bawar and Rawain . The Khasas have played a significant role in the development of wooden architecture of Uttarakhand, as they are known for their skills as wood-carvers. A review of the area wise centres would be helpful for the further discussion to follow.

The survey of the various centres of Jaunsar-Bawar and Rawain has revealed that most of the evidences of wood-carving can still be witnessed in the religious structures, whether old or newly renovated, while on the other hand, the residential houses show either simple or scant designs on their wooden fronts or plain architectural devices. Only rarely few exceptions have come to our notice where the wooden structure of the entrance and/ or the balcony with its arched openings and windows still preserve the traditional old specimens of wood carving. Perhaps for economic considerations (involving high cost of the material and the labor) as well as change of the taste of the people in favor of the modern amenities and styles, are the factors responsible for this phenomenon.

JAUNSAR-BAWAR

The main centres of wood carving in the Jaunsar-Bawar are Hanol, Zadi, Lakhwar, Lakhamandal and Kuna. Hanol (1429 m.) situated on the left bank of river Tons, is the main and the most famous centre having the temple dedicated to the chief tribal god — Mahasu *devata*. Rather, it is the virtual head quarter of the Mahasu-cult of the natives of the entire western Uttarakhand including the adjoining area of Himachal Pradesh. According to a local legend Botha Mahasu, the eldest of the four brothers, along with Chalda Mahasu, after killing the carnivorous demon Kirmar and his associates, "became the ruler of the whole of hill tract."[1]. Supremacy of the divine authority of the deity at Hanol is still recognised by the natives of this region for final decision. Botha Mahasu stays at Hanol only while Chalda Mahasu rotates from village to village on occasions. Built on the original stone structure of cella of an old *Nagar* style temple (the latter's cella is still visible at the rear of the temple) its major portion except the walls is made of exquisitely carved wood.

Approachable by road via Kalsi, Chakrata and Tuni, Hanol is situated deep in the Tons valley at a distance of 180 km from Dehradun. All the wood work has been elaborately done few years ago when the old temple was renovated. The wooden components have a mixture of wood carving — some done in the indigenous folk style but, we also witness others rendered in the popular classical style.

Hanol's main habitat mainly consists of the simple shops cum-residential structures lining the road leading to the temple-campus which have come up for the tourists and the devotees. A short distance away from Hanol towards the north another temple dedicated to Chalda Mahasu stands on a low spur across the Tons at Thadiyar village. But it falls under Rawain region administratively.

At Zadi, situated above a slope on the road from Chakrata to Tuni has an old wooden temple of Mahasu *devata*. While some old wood carving have been noticed on its wooden components betraying the folk tradition, strangely, on its front wooden wall the figures of Hanuman and Durga show realistic figures often seen in the contemporary prints. The latter are recent works, perhaps done during renovation of the temple some time back.

An old multi-tiered pyramidal temple at Kuna has revealed a unique treasure of indigenous wood carvings of great significance. Dedicated to Basik *devata* in the village situated at a distance of 21 km. from Hanol on a subsidiary road branching off from Kanda village. The centre possesses a rich gallery of distinct indigenous art of wood-carving.

Lakhamandal is another important centre which historically and culturally has yielded great wealth of ancient heritage. It has been an important *teerth* of religious importance in the ancient past and is traditionally believed to have been the seat of *lakshagriha* where the Kauravs had mischievously planned to burn alive the Pandavs in the house of shellac (*lakshagriha*). The surviving old temple has revealed some typical wood carvings. Lakhamandal stands at a short distance across Yamuna on the national highway to Yamnotri.

Lakhwar is another centre which is accessible by road from Mussoorie through Kempty village to Chakrata and Tuni, bifurcating mid way towards north. The old wood work has been replaced by the new work done by craftsmen of

Saharanpur. On the other side of the Tons river near Hanol (1429 m.), the famous temple dedicated to Chalda Mahasu *devta* is located at Thadiyar, though administratively it falls under Rawain region.

RAWAIN REGION

Rawain region, extending to the north and north-east of Jaunsar-Bawar is an extension of the same trible culture and religion as the latter's. The main centres of wood carving in Rawain region are Thadiyar, Khasarsali, Sankri, Pujaili, Naitwar, Than, Saur, Arakot, Chinwa, Devalsari and Deorah. A temple bearing thematic carvings on its wooden gate, dedicated to Chalda Mahasu is located at Thadiyar village across river Tons in South-western part of Rawai. It was recently constructed in the traditional Pahari style and inaugurated in 2003. Thadiyar can be reached via, Hanol, covering the distance on foot across Tons. Kharsali is the last village accessible by an uphill bridle path in the north-easterly direction, branching off the Yamnotri route and is not much far from Yamnotri which lies to its north beyond a southward towering spur of the Himalaya.

Situated approximately 45 km away from Barkot, there is a steep uphill track of about 5 kilometers from the main road upto this last village on this side of the border. It is located on a high altitude and receives heavy snowfall in the winters. There are two temples at Kharsali, both dedicated to Someshwar Mahadev. One is gable-roofed and the other is a tower temple also strangely known as the temple of *Shani-devata*, though Shani is neither the presiding nor the subsidiary deity at this temple.

Specimens of wood carving are also found at Raghunath temple at Pujaili. Built in traditional Pahari style, it is situated off the Naugaon-Rajgarhi bus route running towards the left, at a distance of about 15 kilometers from Barkot.

Situated at the confluence of the rivers Rupin and Supin, Netwar, is situated at an altitude of 1401 meters and can be reached from Hanol via Mori. From the main road, one has to walk a short distance down the hill to approach the village.

The village Than is approachable by the Barkot-Hanuman Chatti motor road. But one has to cross a plain stretch of rugged land of about one and a half kilometer across Yamuna river and then climb the 3 kilometers steep slope of the hill on the other side of the river. The village is situated on a flat stretch of land with one traditional old temple and another small new one just behind the former. Specimens of wood carving exist on the gable-roofed traditional temple.

Another important centre of wood work in the Rawain region is Chinwa. It can be approached from Tuni across river Tons via Arakot by taking up a journey on the Tuni-Rohru (H.P.) road. It is situated at an altitude of 1087 metres. There is an old temple dedicated to Pawasi *devata* at Chinwa. The temple once had a very antique wood work executed on the architectural components of the original old temple's exterior. It is now being replaced by a new structure. The old wooden panels with fine carvings have been removed and most of them destroyed by the villagers due to utter ignorance of the aesthetic and historical significance of the artifacts. The temple, when visited by the author in February 2011, was undergoing renovation giving it a new character. However, richly ornamented new wooden door of the temple bears thematic wood carvings based on Hindu mythology rendered in local folk style.

Arakot is situated in the north-west of Uttarakashi district, on the eastern bank of river Pabar beyond Tuni across Tons. It has a tower-type temple dedicated to Kuan *devata*, where wood carving can be noticed on some architectural wooden components. The temple is of recent origin.

Devalsari is situated at a distance of 99 kilometers from Dehradun on Dehradun-Barkot motor route approachable through a subsidiary road towards the right. There is a temple dedicated to Rudreshwar Mahadev which can be approached after half a kilometer walk on the downward slope leading to the temple, almost at the lower end of the village.

The above mentioned places are the main centres of wood carvings in Jaunsar–Bawar and Rawain regions, where we found that it is the religious edifices which have yielded the major part of the specimens of wood carving, though evidences of minor wood–carvings have also been observed, though rarely, in secular architecture at places. The main reason could be that *deodar* wood is considered as the sacred material for the temples, therefore wood, despite being very costly, is still employed as a major component in the construction or renovation of the temples but there is no such customary boundation for the secular architecture, which, of late and now-a-days, is being replaced by use of cement and bricks, as often observed by the author during the field work.

The new developments, specially with the construction of morotrable road in the interior of the region, have rendered supply of these construction material easily available even in the far off areas of the hills, as well as a change of taste and habits of the natives with increased mobility and socio-cultured interaction with the modern urban life of the plains.

Besides, the new restrictions on the felling of trees in the hills with the depleting forests, has made wood a very costly raw-material. Even in the temples which are renovated or reconstructed, despite the fact that the natives are retaining the traditional features of Pahari architecture, use of stone, bricks and cement is gradually replacing the wood, as noticed at some centres in the recent survey. Yet, it has been observed that, traditionally, it has been a common practice among the natives since ancient times to decorate the religious structures in particular with carved designs and thematic motifs on the wooden components, to propitiate the god/s enshrined there. It has been found everywhere since the ancient times that in maters of religious faith the devotees have been offering the best and the purest, irrespective, of the cost element, to their gods as a mark of deep reverence as well as to ensure god's/ goddess's continued blessing, protection and favour. Hence the specimens of wood carving are still witnessed in the centres more in the religious edifices of worship in comparison to the secular ones despite the former's escalated cost.

References

1. Thakur, M. R., *Myths, Rituals and Beliefs in Himachal Pradesh* (Indus Publishing Co., New Delhi, 1997) pp. 69,70.

4

Wood Carving in the Garhwal Himalaya

THEMATIC DEPICTION IN WOOD CARVING : RELIGIOUS ARCHITECTURE

GENERAL INTRODUCTION

The most venerated deity of the entire Janusar-Bawar and Rawain regions of Uttarakhand, is Mahasu *devata.* During the survey of the region, the author found majority of the temples here dedicated to the deity. The cult of Mahasu *devata*, is believed to have reached this region of central Himalaya from the northern ranges of Greater Himalaya, more specifically from Kashmir. Mahasu is originally a non- Brahamanical cult, having its own pantheology, though gradually he also came to be associated with the manifestation of tantric form of Shiv. Mahasu *devata* was a native god of Kashmir. The cult of Mahasu *devata* is believed to have penetrated Jaunsar-Bawar region about four or five hundred years ago.[1] Though the cult is obviously a Hindu cult but it is not the traditional Brahmanical in context, in which the former is understood.

Vedic Brahmanism of the Vedic period (1500 BC to 500 BC) is considered to be historical predecessor of Hinduism.

Pauranic Hinduism is the further evolution of the former. Vedic religion is believed to have been evolved into *Vedant* — the essence of the *Vedas*. The traditions which supported *Vedant* in its formative period came to be considered as *Astika*, which included Hinduism, which in turn incorporated religious beliefs and cults, *Purans* (Sanskrit scriptures), the classical school of Hindu philosophy, different branches of Hinduism – Shaivism, Vaishnavism, Bhaktism, Shaktism and Srauta tradition, basically all have maintained much of the essential form of the vedic religion. According to Encyclopaedia Britanica, "The great epic *Mahabharata* represents the attempt of Vedic Brahminism to adjust itself to the new circumstances reflected in the process of the organization (integration of Aryan beliefs, practices, and institutions) of the various non-Aryan communities."[2]

Garhwal Himalaya is known for the worship of the Mahasu *devata*. In his *Gazetteer of Garhwal Himalaya*, H.G. Walton writes, "The orthodox among the immigrate Brahmans and Rajputs worship the five great gods – Vishnu, Shiv, Devi, the sun and Ganesh. The Khasiyas perform their orisons to the mountain god Shiv chiefly, and the Doms propitiate not only the early local gods who flourished before the advent of the Brahmanic dispensation, but also the multitudinous demons of a later imagination."[3] He further renders vital information: "In Garhwal the temple of Shiv greatly outnumber those dedicated to Vishnu."[4] Initially, the Khasas, are believed to have been worshipers of the Vedic god Rudra. There was a practice among these to make offerings of stones to turn away the difficulties imposed by risky mountain tracks, blizzards or snow storms, in their favor. Later, Vedic god Rudra came to be related to the classical god Shiv. Shiv–Rudra temple at the confluence of the rivers Mandakini and Alaknanda,[5] bear testimony to the fact.

"There we have indisputable written records of at least 5,000 years old that the whole Uttarakhand region was a stronghold of Vedic culture."[6] It was a cradle of the vedic *rishi-munis* and their hermitages were centres where training in performing Vedic rites and rituals was imparted.

Archaeological evidences regarding existence of Vedic culture in ancient period, in Rawain region of Garhwal Himalaya, have also been unearthed. "Moreover, excavations conducted by a team of archaeologist of the Garhwal University in the year 1986-87, under the leadership of K.P. Nautiyal at Purola in the Yamuna Valley, on the banks of the river Kanal, tributary of Yamuna in Uttarkashi, have brought to light that the Kuninda King Amoghabhuti (100-60 BCE) performed an *Asvamegha* sacrifice to commemorate the liberation of this land from the clutches of Greeks, viz. from Spolodotus, the grandson of Menander."[7] The excavation revealed a sacrificial altar in the shape of a flying eagle and cistern (kund), and some coins of Amoghabhuti. "It need no elaboration that the above-mentioned evidences are enough to prove that the Kunind rulers, who ruled this part of the country from 200 BCE to CE 200 were staunch followers of the Vedic tradition along with their ritualistic practices. As such it may be said that during the Kunind ascendancy the whole region of western Uttarakhand was under the sway of vedic culture and Brahmanical religion, and there were brahmans who were well-versed in the sphere of vedic rituals."[8] Besides during Kunind and Paurav rulers of this region also vedic culture was deep rooted.

Shaivism in the region received a setback due to growing influence of Buddhism. The history of Buddhism in Uttarakhand can be traced back to the life span of Buddha who is believed to have visited Uishirdhvaj mountain on the bank of the Ganga in the south of Uttarakhand. Kalsi is known for its Ashok edict (272-236 BCE) and reference of this region occurs in the Buddhist scripture *Ashokavadara*, which proves that this region came under the influence of Buddhism. In circa 5-4 cent B.C. Buddhist monasteries had been established at Ahogang near Kankhal.[9]

Revival of Brahmanical religion in this region owes its debts to the visit of Sankrachary who injected a new soul in the erstwhile lost glory of Brahmanical cult. He established Jyotirmath or Joshimath monastery and restored the temple of Naryan at Badri. From Badri he left for Kedar, where he died at the age of thirty two. He introduced the worship of Vishnu.

The Brahmanical cult of the region, especially among the indigenous people, lost its erstwhile popularity and following owing to the advent of Mahasu cult from Kashmir in the present area of study. According to a popular belief prevalent in the region, Vishnu was defeated in a battle by Mahasu and thus the former was given a secondary place.[10]

Mahasu *devata* were four deities known as Basik, Pibasak (Pawasi), Buthiya or Baitha (Botha) and Chalta or Chalda. In the legends prevalent related to the deities some variations can be observed.

According to Walton Una Bhat lived with his large family and relatives in a village called Maindrath. Kirbir Dana (*danav* or demon) used to eat one of his family members daily until Una with his three sons and one daughter escaped to the forests of the Yamuna. One night Mahasu *Devta* appeared in his dream and advised him to proceed to Kashmir where the four Mahasus dwelt and to destroy Kirbir *Dana* with their help. Thus Una went to Kashmir and came to the place where Mahasu's watchman lay asleep. He woke him up and addressed him as *mama* (maternal uncle). Being pleased by his address the watchman told him about the way to Mahasu through the forest of Ghagli and Kanani Tal in Kashmir. Una followed the watchman's instructions and on reaching the abode of Mahasu appealed to them to help him. Mahasu assured him to destroy Kirbir. Chalda Mahasu gave him a handful of rice, an earthen vessel and his staff. Una was told to strike the staff on the earth causing water to come out and to prepare rice for himself. This would also ensure that Mahasu's favour was with him. He was asked to throw some of the rice into the Tons to prevent Kirbir from causing any harm to Una. He was also told to plough his field after employing a heifer to his yoke and ensure that the plough was driven by a bachelor only. By doing so the plough would turn into gold and his share will turn into silver. On the five furrows ploughed by him, he would find five stone idols of the four Mahasus and their mother, Deolari. Una did as he was instructed. In the first furrow appeared Basik with his thigh transfixed. Pawasi appeared with a wounded ear and Botha with an injured eye. Chalda appeared inact and thus is able to roam whereas the other three are found only in the temples dedicated to them. Una's youngest son became a Deopujari, his second son became a Rajput and the third became a musician. Kirbir *Dana* was killed by Kalu Bir, the attendant of Mahasu and his head was hung up by him in the temple of Mahasu. Garhwal became a seat of Basik and Pawasi and Jaunsar- Bawar that of Botha and Chalda. There are temples dedicated to Sangru at Mandhan in Khats Koru and Udpalta, where he is carried about *khats* Semalta, Udpalta, Koru and Seli. There is a temple dedicated to Chalda at Thadiyar, in district Uttarkashi of Rawain region.

O.C. Handa also mentions a similar legend but with slight variation.[11] According to him the man who lived in Bawar was Huna Bhat. Out of his seven sons, six were consumed by the demon Kirbir. About Huna's dream he writes that he saw four great warriors who were in the army of the king of Kashmir and that with their help he would kill Kirbir. Instead of any watchman, a Brahmin of Hatkoti, named Naga directed him the way to Kashmir. When he started his journey he abruptly felt very light and filled with energy and vigour. His eye blinked and the next moment he found himself standing near a water spring. Mahasu *Devta* was supposed to live beneath this water spring. When a divine being guarding the spring, who was the wazir of Mahasu *Devata* called Shedkulia, appeared before Huna. He addressed him as *mama*. The rest of the legend is much like the one mentioned by Walton. Names of the four Mahasus mentioned by Handa are Basik (Vasuki,), Pawasi, Botha and Chalda. Hanol became the seat of Botha.

Beside the four Mahasus, their pantheon comprises of their polyandrous wife, Natari and their mother Deoladi, The Mahasus have four attendants called *birs* —Kapal, Kaulu, Kailath (Kaniasana) and Shedkulia. They in turn have four *bolyaninis* meaning female helpers, who reside at Daraghat below Tuni. There is a temple which is dedicated to Deoladi at Maindrath.

Madhu Jain mentions two legends, one is the same as told aboe, while the other is diffeent.[12]. According to the latter, at the beginning of Kalyug people of Uttarakhand were tortured by demons. The most powerful among them, Kirmar, devoured all the seven sons of the Huna *Rishi.* The demon wanted to have the wife of Huna named Kirtak. The *Rishi* prayed to Shiv to protect her. Thus Shiv punished the demon by making him blind. Then they evoked the Hateshwari *Devi* of Hatkoti, *ashtbhuji* Durga. The latter asked them to go to Kashmir and to seek Lord Shiv's favour by offering him prayer which they did. Shiv was pleased and assured them to destroy the demons. Rishi was also asked to appease the *Devi* with rituals and prayers on his return. Consequently the goddess appeared encircled with flames and gods appeared from different parts of her body. According to the prediction made by Lord Shiv the four gods were to appear who are known as the Mahasu who killed the demons.

Mahasu *Devata* might be a Nag deity as per another legend related to Brahmanical tradition which alludes its origin to the latter.[13] According to this, a man was ploughing field in the pargana Bucan, when abruptly a snake appeared before him and told him that he was sent by the divinity called Mahasu *Devata* and asked him to install his idol. Further that it would reveal to him the laws that were to be obeyed. In this legend enunciated by Hamilton and quoted by Walton, there is no reference to the four deities known as the Mahasus. About another legend Walton writes that Una was told by the watchman that after crossing the forest of Ghagti "He would next reach Kanani Tal, the lake of Kanana, into which he was to spit and throw some of his hair. If his saliva turned into *cowries* and his hair into snakes, he would know that he was in the miracle-working land of Kashmir"[14]. Here again we get reference of snakes.

O.C. Handa believes that Mahasu had originally been a *Nag* deity in Kashmir"[15] He points to similarity between 'Mahasu' and Bhagsu *Nag* near Dharmsala and believes that Mahasu brothers are collectively known as *Nag-Chauth*. As per legend mentioned by him as soon as Huna Brahmin blinked he instantly reached a water spring under which Mahasu *Devata* was supposed to live. According to Handa Mahasu had been originally a *Nag* deity.[16]

Mahasu is also believed to be a tantric manifestation of Maha Shiv.[17] This probability cannot be denied. Socio-cultural history is replete with such examples when the original names got transformed and their *apabhramsa* forms became popular. Besides, *nag* or a serpent is often depicted with Shiv[18] and the *nag* element is 8present in the Mahasu cult, suggesting some link between these two deities.

Delving deep into the various aspects related to Mahasu cult and examining pros and cons associated with its origin, it can be assumed that Mahasus were the native local deities of Kashmir which reached Uttarakhand approximately four or five hundred years ago. The entire Himalaya region being natural habitat of snakes and reptile creatures, which the indigenous residents of the region must have been encountering often infusing awe and terror due to their dangerous and harmful nature at times, it must have been the main factor of *nag* or snakes being raised to the seat of veneration. As the heavenly land of Kashmir abounds in water springs, consequently, water spring and snake (the former being the favorite place to be visited by the latter) must have come to be associated with the cult of Mahasu *devatas*. As snake also adorns the neck of Shiv who resides in the highest heavenly abode of Himalayan region, it was natural that affinities were drawn between the former and Mahasu.

Thus the Mahasu cult, a native cult of Kashmir, found extensive popularity in the western Himalayan range. Popularity, so far it is associated with a deity, also denotes its power and strength, its infinite and enternal potential to fulfill and grant the wishes of its followers and also of its power to emancipate their sufferings. Since Mahasu cult had its roots in the soil of Himalaya it must have appealed with greater acceptability to the other indigenous folk of the mountaineous areas.

As the Mahasu *devata* fulfilled the wish of Una Brahmain of Maindrath, saving his family and villagers from Kirbir Dana (demon) by destroying the latter, it possessed greater power and strength for the indigenous folk of Uttarakhand than the earlier presiding deity of the temple located in their vicinity — lord Vishnu at Hanol. According to Walton, in the area of our study, Shankaracharya, "On the expulsion or conversion of the Buddhists he introduced the worship of the god Vasudev or

Basdeo, a form of Vishnu.[19] Eventually, the great faith of the native folk in their own familiar god of the mountains must have led them to replace the erstwhile presiding deity with Mahasu *devata*. Consequently, the stone sculptures of the deities of Nagar temples were removed from the cella, giving place to the face-images of Mahasu *devata* and to the pantheology associated with the deity. The Nagar style of cella of Mahasu temple at Hanol and the stone sculptures of Vishnu lying in the precincts outside bear testimony to this fact. There are other temple-sites in Rawain region where stone sculptures of the Brahamnical gods/goddesses like Ganesh, Vishnu, Mahisasura-mardini and others were seen by the author lying astray in the vicinity of the present wooden temples.

Even if we take into consideration Mahasu as manifestation of Shiv, as claimed by some scholars and authors, the need to raise it to the greater and more powerful manifestation of Shiv must have been felt later since Shaivism, once a popular cult have in earlier times, was superseded by Buddhism. Hence when the Shaivaite cult was rejuvenated, more powerful prefix, (*Maha*) was added to it and, the cult (Mahashiv) might have come to be considered to be a synonym of Mahasu.

This has been observed during my survey at few places. For example, at the Pokhu *devata* temple at Naitwar, on the eastern side of the temple wall on the wooden plank under the roof is inscribed '*Mahasu Devata hi Mahashiv hai*' (Mahasu *Devata* is Mahashiv). At Thadiyar during my enquiry and discussion with the priest present there the latter asserted that the deity (Mahasu) is Mahashiv. Thus we find the tendency of a synthesis of the indigenous religious beliefs and deities of the natives of Jaunsar-Bawar and Rawain region and the traditional Brahminical pantheology and notions, getting mixed with the native Mahasu cult.

However, one cannot rule out the Mahasu cult having its own indigenous roots features and characteristics which attributed distinct existence and identify to it as cult. Especially noteworthy is the pantheology of this deity. The Mahasus are actually the four brothers – Botha with transfixed thigh, Pawasi with a wounded ear. Botha with an injured eye and Chalda intact and able to roam about. Further, they also have a polyandrous wife Natari and their mother Deoladi.

So far as the temple architecture is concerned, prolific depiction of the Brahmanical themes taken from *Ramayan, Mahabharat* and *Pauranic* sources as well as the Hindu gods–goddesses and Brahamanical symbols and motifs found expression. Even prolusory examination of carvings on the wooden architectural components forming part of the decoration on the exterior of the edifices and on the exterior portion of wooden components of the interior bears testimony to this fact.

According to Encyclopaedia Britanica, "Also in the second half of the 1st millennium B.C., the older gods of the Rigveda began to lose ground before Vishnu and Shiva, the first a minor divinity in earlier times, the second fertility gods, perhaps inherited from the pre-vedic Harappa culture with whom the Vedic god Rudra was identified. Local divinities in the areas gradually occupied by Aryan culture were assimilated to one or other of these, and the doctrine of *avataras* or divine incarnations made it possible for theriomorphic gods (gods worshipped in the form of the beast) and divinized heroes to become incarnations of Vishnu. The religion of this period is reflected in the two great epics, the Mahabharat and the Ramayana (q.g.v.), and in the texts on law and human conduct generally called Dharma Sutras and Dharma Shastra. The religious attitude usually known in Indian contexts as *bhakti* (q.v.), or devotion to a personal deity also developed. The new gods were normally worshiped with prayer, offerings of flowers and food, incense or music; the rite of worship (puja) had replaced that of sacrifice (yajna). The most important text of early bhakti is the Bhagavad Gita (q.v.) inserted into the Mahabharat epic as a discourse addressed to the hero Arjuna by the incarnate god Krishna".[20]

The Brahmanical cult in Garhwal Himalaya, though might have got influenced by the growing popularity of Mahasu cult and the local gods and goddesses, yet thematic depiction of episodes drawn from *Mahabharat, Ramayan*, *Purans* etc. on the exterior of the wooden buildings of the region bear testimony to the fact that venerability of the Brahmanical gods, goddesses and popular characters or heroes from the literary Brahmanical texts did not vanish. It enjoyed a consistent existence along with the more popular cult of Mahasus and other local deities in the life and ethos of the natives.

The wood work executed in the wooden temples of Jaunsar-Bawar and Rawain regions of Garhwal Himalaya evinces some very exquisite examples of sonorous craftsmanship. The virtuoso craftsmen of this region work with divine inspiration and follow some does and don'ts especially when they work at the religious buildings. The author had an opportunity to meet the craftsmen at the temple of Karn during an earlier visit in 2002, when the renovation on work was being carried there. The craftsmen involved in the work revealed that after taking bath when they start the work they do not take meals nor smoke till they finish the days work and wear special costumes after bath while carrying out their work at the temple.

The temple of Basika *devata* at Kuna was also visited by the author earlier in 2002 and again recently for a more detailed study regarding the present research work. During the first visit to the site, I was informed by the local landlord Prem Singh

Panwar (age 70 then) in whose campus stands the *Bir's* temple that the artisan who constructed the temple was Bona Badi (बोना बढ़ी) about whom a strange story is traditionally popular and believed to be true by the people, and which has come down to him traditionally in the family from generation to generation. According to this 'Bona' was a particular caste of the artisans and '*Badi*' is for '*barhai*' (carpenter), his profession. Thus, 'Bona Badi' as his popular name became his identify in the village.

According to Prem Singh Panwar Bona Badi, either due to some boon or curse, was gifted with great skill in carving but with the condition attached to it that (generally such things are experienced in a dream or somnipathy) he would never reveal to anybody his secret or the source of inspiration of his extraordinary skill in chiseling exquisite forms in wood. Perhaps he was blessed to work with excellent skill as long as he would not reveal the secret to anybody but also cursed to die if he did so. The villagers curious to know about the secret of his work and skill, once played a trick to compel him to speak, by hiding his chief instrument, the *bashola* (an indigenous axe-cum-chisel). Unable to work without his instrument, fearing the wrath of the *devata* in leaving the work incomplete, he opted for the other option – to speak and die. Also informing of his fate, he asked his wife about the where about of the *bashola* also revealing the truth about his skill. As soon as he spoke he breathed his last. Legends grew about the life and work of the gifted people. Perhaps this might have been one example immortalizing the excellent carvings done in wood there.

Noteworthy in this context in popular Jaunsari story which unearths the extraordinary skill of the indigenous craftsmen in executing carving work in wood and also tells us how liquor or its local equivalent was invented.

According to this story after death human beings were taken to hell or heaven depending upon their deeds in this life. They were escorted by *Jims*, (the messenger- soldiers of Lord *Jimraj*, i.e., *Yamraj* — the god of death). When came the turn of the carpenter, *Jimraj* sent two *Jims* to fetch him. The craftsman had already made a twenty story house inside a large tree trunk, which in itself was a wonder. He lured the *Jims* to have a glimpse of his exquisite craftsmenship before taking him to *Jimraj*. When they were having the look at its interior, they were lost in the admiration of the craftstman's skill. As they reached the topmost floor, the carpenter cleverly locked them and also shut all the twenty doors one by one. Thus it became impossible for the *Jims* to come out and they went missing.

When *Yamraj* came to know that his *Jims* had got missing during their task of fetching the carpenter, the former made every possible enquiry. The carpenter cancealed his role in the disappearance of the *Jims*. Consequently, on *Yamraj's* order, his workers developed an intoxicating substance, on consuming which a person would loose restrain on his nerves and would reveal the truth boastfully. The team thus invented liquor. The substance was called '*soor*' or '*soora*'. (*Yamraj* then arranged a dinner at the village where the carpenter lived, where *soora* was also served amply. Thus everyone started boasting of his/her achievements, in their respective field. The carpenter also became under the *soora's* influence and revealed the truth about the twenty storeyed house in a tree trunk, where the two *Jims* had been locked.

Such legends might have been woven in a hyperbolic manner about the extraordinary skills of some carpenters or wood carvers to stress the level of perfection of the artisans. It also bears testimony to the fact that wood was the only medium and primary raw material which was employed by the indigenous folk in ancient times for the houses.

BRAHMANINCAL THEMES

Ramayan Sources

Among the thematic depictions carved on the wooden components of the religious edifices taken from the life of Lord Rama or other Brahamincal texts profusely find manifestation generally on their exterior. Reference to the Rawain region in context of the holy river Bhagirathi flowing through and bringing florescence in the socio-cultural life of this area is found in *Srimad Valmikiya Ramayan*. The river is named after the king Bhagirath who, according to legend, performed penance at Gokarntirth for one thousand years to bring the Ganga on the earth.

Brahma pleased with Bhagirath's penance blessed him with the boon:

"Iyam cha dubita jyeshtha tab Ganga Bhavishyati,
Twakriten cha namnath loke sthasyati vishruta. ||5||"[21]

Thus Ganga came to be regarded as the eldest daughter of Bhagirath after his name as Bhagirathi.

"Ganga tripathga nam divya Bhagirathiti cha,
Trin patho bhavayantiti tasyat tripathga smrit. ||6||" [22]

According to D.D. Sharma : "The author of the Ramayana too seems to have not only an acquaintance with the Himavata region, but with its inhabitants as well. In the context of the search for Sita while dispatching his vanaras, Sugriva instructs them to search her in the *Himavat* region which was inhabited by different ethnic groups of that period. In the Ram. (Kiskin. 40:21) there is a mention of the Yamuna mountain, the source of the river Yamuna. Again in the Yudhakand (74:31) there is a detailed description of the mount "Ausadhi Parvata" which is said to be situated in between the mount Rsabha and Kailas. It is said to be the mountain from where Hanuman took sanjivani, the life-giving herb to save the life of Lakshmana,. Similarly (in the *Bal- sarga* 43), we find a mention of some of the important rivers of the region, viz. Bhagirathi/Jahanvi and Kalindi (Yamuna) (Also see Ram, 1:24: 1;35: 13-23; 37; VI:74:74:26-28; 101:32-42 etc.)"[23]

The exemplary life and deeds of Lord Ram found venerability in this region of Jaunsar-Bawar and Rawain as evident from the wood carvings of the exposed components of the wooden temples where in thematic depiction, *Ramayan,* and Sri *Ramchatrimanas* had been vital sources and the legacy of the Brahmincal tradition.

The most venerated temples of Mahasu *devata* located at Hanol in Jaunsar-Bawar region is an outstanding example of profusely rendered wood-carving having promiscuous thematic depictions derived from varied sources of Brahmincal origin The wooden façade of the main entrance of the temple has carvings in low relief depicting scenes taken from *Ramayan* along with other from different religious literary sources.

The façade has an arched wooden door-frame , having three door jambs set in recession. These are carved with panels having scenes from *Ramayan*, depicted in narrative manner. The figures against white background in bright colours, each divided from the other by a projected wooden stripe painted brown. This renders the scenes with the sense of high relief and also evokes the feeling of prolix space and time.

The central and the lower door jams have scenes exclusively taken from *Ramayan*. The trio of Ram, Laxhman, and Sita in exile appears twice . A panel on central door jambs on the left side is carved with Sita holding a *varmala* in her raised hands in front of Ram indicating the scene at *swayambar* . The central door jamb on the right side has a scene where Lord Ram, seated on a modern type of wooden chair, is handing over his ring to Hanuman standing in front of him. On the lower door jamb on the right side Hanuman again appears with clasped hands in reverance in front of Sita seated under the tree in Ashok *vatika*. Adjacent to it on the central door jamb appears Ravan's wife Mandodari with her hands placed on the left leg of ten-headed. Ravan pleading him to return Sita with all her dignity to Ram. The scene is the literal representation of the following text of *Ramcharita-manas* (*Sundarkand*):

रहसि जोरि कर पति पग लागी। बोली बचन नीति रस पायी ।।
कंत करज हरि सन परिटरट्। मोहर कहा अति हित हिय धरयू।।
समुझत जासु दूत कइ करनी। स्तवहिं गर्भ रजनीचर धनी।।
तासु नारि निज सचिव बोलाई। पठवहु कंत जो चहहुभलाई।।[24]

That is, with folded hands, touching Rawan's feet Mandodari appeals to Ravan to give up animosity with Ram reminding him that if the thought of the latter's messenger (Hanuman) can cause abortion of the pregnant women by his very thought how great could be the prowess of his master (Ram), The artist however is not oblivious of the royal surrounding of the palace as noticed by the details carved in the background – a door and a coloumn with folds of the curtain. The scene apparently is inspired by *Ramacharitmanas* of Tulsidas since Balmiki's *Ramayan*, does not mention such conservation between Ravan and Mandodari. A reference to this is available in the latter when, though after Ravan had been killed by the former, it mentions Mandodari lamenting over Ravan's death saying she had pleaded him to relinquish animosity with Lord Ram and that he did not listen to her advice:

क्रियतामविरोध व राघवेणेति यन्मथा ।।18।।
उच्यमानो न ग हासि तस्येयं व्युटिरागता।[25]

Noteworthy in this regard is the appearance of Goswami Tulsidas, the author of *Shri Ramcharitmanas,* on the lower most panel of the central door-jamb. His left leg is placed on the right one as he sits cross-legged, with left hand placed on his left leg, and his right. hand resting on the other leg is holding a rosary. Donning a round cap with a red pompon hanging at back and has an open book in his front. His posture, his placement within the space with a tree at the back and his face in profile whereas the body with profile face in three-quarter pose, all bear close resemblance to the depiction of Goswami Tulsidas in the popular contemporary prints.

The other scenes witnessed on these door jambs are - *Lanka-dahan,* Ram's army crossing the ocean, unconscious Laxman lying on ground after being hit by *Virghatini shakti* (arrow), annihilation of five commanders — Virupaksh, Yupakash, Durdhar, Pradhas and Bhaskaran of Ravan's army by Hanuman, (the reference to it occurs in *Sundarkand* of Balmiki *Ramayan* showing their severed hands. Two females in front (one enthroned and the other kneeling in front) are craftsman's own imagination since they have no literary reference. Another scene carved here shows Hanuman flying over Ayodhya with the mountain containing *sanjivani* (life-saving herbal plant) while Bharat, mistaking him to be *rakshas* (demon) aims with his arrow at the former. A panel depicts a female in red costume holding and lamenting over a severed head (possibly of Indrajit, killed by Lakshman). A crowd of people is shown mourning his demise. Another scene depicts Lord Ram aiming his arrow at the ten-headed Ravan . It is interesting to note the apt utilization of the space by the craftsman on the narrow horizontal portion below the pediment of the porch leading to the temple. The scene of crossing of ocean by *vanar sena* (an army of monkies) of Lord Ram is carved on this portion. The *setu* or the bridge is almost like a contemporary suspensim bridge as seen at Lakshman Jhulla in Rishikesh . In this panel appears a monkey at regular intervals until they reach Lanka depicted on the left side. On the right, interestingly, a vertical series of one monkey with a weapon in hand mounting over another is depicted in a stereo type manner on the extreme right. It seems to be the depiction of an event at Ravan's palace though no palace-architecture is noticed. Ten-headed Rawan is seated with his hands held by Hanuman on his right, delivering lord Ram's message, with another figure in similar pose on his left. Adjacent to the latter, most probably, is a figure of *muni* with a hand raised in *abhaya mudra*, seated on a chair. The chair is akin to the plastic chairs of the recent times so popular and easily available in market, betraying the contemporary influence on it. Lanka on the left side is represented by few small building structures and some soldiers and residents of the town. The 'crossing of ocean by *vanar sena* is a novel way of solving the problem of space and the carver's creative approach also revealing modern impact on the wood carving of the region. The wood carving at the temple of Mahasu *devata* at Hanol was done by Gangaram for eleven years, from 1984 to 1995, as informed by him during our recent meeting at Chinwa.

The temple of Mahasu at Lakhwar, in Jaunsar-Bawar region is another site of exquisite wood work . The present temple is newly built structure which bears resemblance to a Buddhist pagonda style of religious architecture. Earlier an old temple dedicated to the same deity existed here, a photo of which can be seen hanging in the hall on the ground floor. The two cellas where the deities are placed on either sides of a conference room are located on the second floor. The temple (cella) adjacent to the staircase is dedicated to Botha Mahasu *devata* while the other one on the other end of the floor is dedicated to Chalda

Mahasu. The arched wooden door-way of the temple of Botha Mahasu *devata* is carved with some scenes of *Ramayan* derivation, viz., Jayant in the form of crow (Lord Indra's son) biting Sita's feet to test the strength of Lord Ram, whom the latter killed with an arrow. Sita crouches at the bite. The crow is carved with unusually elongated neck, rather giving an impression of it being a swan. Bali-Sugriv *Yudhha* (battle), Lord Ram giving his ring to Hanuman as a mark of his identity to Hanuman (his messenger), Ravan with the projectiles held in hand, Sursa preventing Hanuman from entering Lanka, Lav and Kush with Sita and *rishipatni* or an attendant are some other themes from the epic in wood showing Brahmanical sources. All chiseled wooden architectural components were made by the carvers at Saharanpur and transported to the site for being fitted into their respective places as per the architectural design of the temple by the locals. However the original building of the temple was in *Pahari* style entirely constructed with local material and skill.

The striking feature which makes the temple of Mahasu *devata* at Lakhwar stand apart from other traditional wooden temples in Garhwal Himalaya is the modern imported carvings from the plains.

The temple's architectural design is apparently influenced by the Buddhist Pagoda type temple architecture. A marked change is noticed in the main deity which is made of white marble commonly seen in the modern Hindu temples, which is in contrast to the traditional practice of installing face-images of metal (brass) or silver.[26]

The temple of Chalda Mahasu *devata* at Thadiyar was constructed between 1998 to 2002 and the main craftsman associated with construction and wood carving of this canopied composite roofed temple is the well known craftsman of Uttarakhand, Gangaram. The author had visited the site earlier in October 2002, when construction of the temple was nearing completion. It again has been revisited recently. The erstwhile richly carved arched wooden door frame of the temple has now been painted with golden colour. Among the scenes carved on the arched wooden door jambs are the same episodes from Ramayan, namely, Sita in Ashoka *vatika*, the trio Ram, Lakshman and Hanuman, Ram's handing over his ring to Hanuman, Ravan trying to threaten Sita in Ashok *vatika*, dropping of Lord Rama's ring by Hanuman from Ashok tree for Sita, Lord Ram and Sita exchanging garland at the *swayambar* after the former had broken the Shiv's bow, reclining ten-headed Ravan as he is informed by two attendants about the arrival of Ram's army in Lanka. (their gestures of conveying the information are very expressive), unconscious Laxman in the lap of Lord Ram after being hit by *shakti ban* with monkeys around and Hanuman flying over Ayodhya with a mountain containing *sanjivni* etc., which have been noticed in Hanol and Thadiyar.

The two sets of carving bear close resemblance, naturally since the same was also engaged in the construction of the Mahasu *devata* temple at Deovan during 1970-73 and Mahasu *devata* temple at Devali during 1975-1980. His contribution in the construction or renovation of the wooden temples of Jaunsar-Bawar and Rawain regions is awesome, exemplary and outstanding. The aged craftsman was interviewed by the author at the site of the temple of Pawasi *devata* at Chinwa during her recent visit of the centre and also saw him engaged in carving the themes on wooden panels. It is unfortunate that the temple is losing its erstwhile, original form and the antique wood work rendered in an original and unique style of its own. It will be discussed later at the end of this chapter.

The arched door frame of the temple of Kaun *devata* at Arakot has individual Brahmanical deities carved on it but no scene taken from *Ramayan* finds manifestation except one showing Hanuman seated cross leged with a mace in hand.

The study of the wood carvings of temple of Pawasi *devata* at Chinwa, encounters with the drastic consequences the wooden temples of the hilly area are facing due to ongoing reconstruction work and losing their antique wood carvings due to sheer ignorance of the indigenous folk and also due to non-intervention of the government and ASI in extending protection to these site of great cultural heritage of the hills and lack of efforts to acquire, and preserve such antique and valuable wood work when it is replaced by new ones and is thus evanesced forever, since either the replaced antique wood work is used as fuel by the villagers or left in open to face the adversities of the nature. The reconstruction work at Chinwa is ongoing since 2006, being undertaken by the veteran craftsman of Uttarakhand who has brought florescence in the wood carving of the Jaunsar-Bawar and Rawain region by his continuous contribution. The antique and old wood carvings were well documented by the author and discussed in the book — 'The Wooden Temples of Uttarakhand; A Study of Art and Architecture'. The erstwhile wood work of the temple did not have any wooden panel or component carved with *Ramayan* theme. Partially reconstructed temple of Chalda Mahasu, nevertheless, has wooden components of deodar carved with scenes taken from *Ramayan*. These include Ram aiming with his bow and arrow to punish the ocean, Lord Ram giving his ring to Hanuman for Sita, Hanuman carrying fainted Laxman in his arms, Lord Ram shooting at the golden stag on the request made by Sita, Hanuman in Ashok *vatika*, Hanuman being handed over *Churamani* by Sita whose right hand is in *abhaya mudra*, Ravan's two spies in disguise being caught by Hanuman and were later allowed to go back by Laxman with the message of Lord Ram for Ravan. The scene depicts Laxman holding his bow in right hand and with the left hand stretched asking them to leave. The two spies with folded hands in front, disguised as monkey, Hanuman flying in the sky and a figure below (scene could not be identified). The most interested scene being the one where Lord Ram is depicted aiming with his bow and arrow at ocean depicted with curvy which caused ocean to appear in personified form with folded hands in front of Ram, his form being smaller in size to Ram's . Another noteworthy scene is when Hanuman is depicted in Ashoka *Vatika* climbed on a tree and Sita is seated on its front. The composition being very unusual from the traditional representation where Sita is always, depicted under the tree. All the scenes whether indoor or outdoor, are all set often on a platform-type form each scene being separated by the other by a stripe of geometrical design, corners having stylized ornamental leaf motifs as also seen at Hanol. But they are more ornamental at Chinwa. It is interesting to note the solutions evolved by the craftsman to solve the problem of limited space, imposed by squarish panel dividing the door jambs, by introducing or adding projections, sometimes diagonally or by means of simply introducing a stage-like platform to raise the characters. Noteworthy in this context is the scene wherein Lord Ram is depicted standing erect with his bow in hands and aiming the arrow at the golden stag. The stag has been placed on a triangular platform which ejects from the edge of the panel and the stag with his head turned backward towards Lord Ram, waits for his eternal fate and seems to be standstill.

There is a small wooden temple of *bir* near the temple of Pawasi *devata* at Chinwa which has a wooden porch in front and an arched door way with a single door jamb. Though not much thematic depiction form *Ramayan* is to be observed here, still Hanuman with a mace in partially flying posture with a mountain containing *sanjivani* is carved in the left corner. In the right corner is carved Laxman holding a bow in his hands arming an arrow at Hanuman, mistaking the latter to be a demon. In between the two is the arch crowned by decorative petal motifs. To solve the limitation of space posed by fixed squarish areas available on either side of the arch, the panel is left devoid of any palace or building so commonly depicted in other scenes. Moreover, strickingly enough the size of the mountain being carried by Hanuman in his left hand, has been reduced to a considerable extent. The devices and the mannerism evolved by the indigenous artisans to deal with the limitation of space, are noteworthy and interesting, leading to simplification of the details and by bringing out necessary modifications in the depiction of these stories found in literary sources.

The small gable-roofed temple of Mahasu *devata* at Zadi is another lucrative site from the point of view of wood carving of promiscuous nature having folk as well as modern impact, connatural due to the interaction of the indigenous folk and artisans with the art work, calenders and pictures of religious themes available in the markets in urban areas. The racking cornice of the gable roof is carved with the trio consisting of Lord Ram, Laxman and Sita. Their postures, gestures, costumes, ornaments and the suggestive architectural details at back show close very close resemblance to the prints of these legendary figures available in the market and seem to be a copy of it. The wooden façade of the temple has an image of Hanuman with a mace and a mountain containing *Sanjivani* carved on it and painted with orange, green, yellow, white and black colours. The background has been painted with blue colour. The posture is one which can be visualized in calendar art of the modern times. The horizontal wooden planks supporting the gable roof on the left side of the temple has a medallion with a bust image probably of Lord Ram, very crudely painted. Its colours are almost faded except that of white.

The temple of Kali at Koti-Kanesar in Rawain region has a richly carved and gaudly painted wooden façade with scenes of *Ramayan* derivation, viz., Lord Ram and Lakshman in search of Sita, Hanuman in Ashoka *Vatika* giving Lord Ram's ring to Sita, Annihilation of ten-headed Ravan by Lord Ram. Coronation ceremony of Lord Ram etc. Modern impact is vividly noticed in the depiction of Hanuman who has wide opened his heart to reveal the image of Lord Ram and Sita in it, a popular subject matter of the contemporary times and the posture also inter-osculate with the similar prints available in the market and seem to have been derived from it. The carving lacks refinement.

Mahabharath Source

Eipsodes taken from the epic *Mahabharat*, have also found profuse manifestation in the wood carving of Jaunsar-Bawar and Rawain regions. This region appears to have been familiar with the author of Mahabharat as borne out by references to Uttarakhand. According to D.D. Sharma, "In the Mbh. (Vana.85:88-89) we find mention of the rivers of the region, viz Ganga, the Yamuna, Saraswati, Rathastha (western Ramganga), Sarayu, Gomati and Gandaki, along with several streams of the river Ganga. In the Vena. (68:3) there is a mention of the Yamuna Parvata or Kalindagiri, the source of the rivers Yamuna. Besides the mountains, some of the important river which came in the way of Pandavs, too have found a mention there. These are Yamuna (Vana. 167:1-21), Alaknanda (rbid, 155: 26), Nanda (ibid, 5:2), Aparananda (ibid., 145., 145:13-24), and Kaushiki (ibid 145). Moreover, the famous Badrikasrama too had come into existence there (Vana.110: 121; vide Dabra, 2055: 63,69)" He further elaborates, "In the context of the exilement of Pandavas, their stay in the Ekacakranagar, (identified with Chakrata; Dehradun), in the guise of brahmanas too shows that the authors of the Mbh were well acquainted with various parts of the region. References to the precious Himalayan presents brought by the people of the Himalaya at the time of Rajasuya Yajna (Sabha. 52:2-7), participation of the Himalayan tribes, viz. Khasas. Tanganas, Daradas, and Kulindas in the great war,[43] Arjuna's visit to Indrakila *Parvat*, his fight with Shiva in the guise of Kirata, and acquiring *pasupatastra* from him too are indicators of the same fact."[28]

There is a temple dedicated to Duryodhan at Saur and Karn at Deorah in the Rawain region. Besides, there are festivals commemorating the strength of Kauravs and Pandavs. During the *Devlaang Parv* celebrated at Gangtadi in Rawain, a tall cedar tree is fixed and to this tree a large number of matches are fixed. These are torched after the *pooja* and the devotees get divided into *Sathis* and *Pasis*, i.e., Kauravas and Pandavas respectively. Each group thus formed tries to uproot the cedar tree and to tilt it to its side to prove the strength and power over the opponent.

Close association of Pandavs to this region of Garhwal is borne out by the performative rituals, dances, narratives and plays. All through Garhwal, although there is variation in enactment of *Mahabharat* - episodes performed during the Pandav dance ritual, the ritual of *shraadha* called *Gainda* is universally witnessed from Pindar valley at the eastern border to the Tons valley forming the western boundary of Gahwal.[29] There are references to Uttara Sankelas performing dance and music for the Pandavs when they visited this region. Bhim took the form of Babrubahan locally known as Bhabrik, as an act of penance on a pilgrimage through the valleys and mountains. "The myth is still enacted in the rituals of *Jakh* all through the Alaknanda valley. Equally extensively the ritual is dedicated to the villainous king Kams who is worshipped as Kaansa in the same valley. Dwari, the daughter of Nand and Yashoda, also finds a cult centre in the same valley. The races of Tons valley where the cult of Pandavs and Kauravs coexists in every village, claim that their ancestors had fought for both the Kauravs and Pandavs and hence the worshippers of both."[30]

Thus the indigenous folk living adjacent to Tons river and in Garhwal consider themselves to be the descendants of the Pandavs. Pandav-*Vivah* practiced in the regions near Tons river also supports this belief. "What is particularly intriguing about this region is the acceptance of anti-heroes, Duryodhan, Karn and even Dushasan, as god kings.[31] There is a temple dedicated to Duryodhan at Saur, and a temple dedicated to Karn at Deorah in Rawain region. Besides the natives of Sarnaul in Rawain region consider themselves descendants of Pandavs and Pandav-*Nritya* performed in the region known also with different names in local dialect, viz., *Mandan*, *Mandawana*, *Pandon ki Saraad* etc., is very popular and distinct. During the performance different deities descend on males and females known as Pashwa. These deities include *Nagraja* (Krishna), Khati (Arjuna), Drupata (Draupadi) etc. The dance is based on varied episodes of the epic *Mahabharat,* e.g., the game of dice between the Kauravs and Pandavs, deception and betrayal by the Kauravs, Draupadi's *Cheerharan* and restoration of the kingdom by the Pandavs.

Thus the indigenous folk have reverence for the great heros of *Mahabharat* and the stories of their valour and bravery are sung in the folk lore of the region. After taking into account these socio-historical and religio-cultural evidences, one is led to logical consectary that due to consists occurrence and popularity of the episodes of Mahabharat in the life of the natives, the artisans too had a connatural penchant for depicting these episodes in the wood carvings. The themes of *Mahabharat* origin have been quite popular as noticed in the wood carvings of Jaunsar-Bawar and Rawain regions.

The temple of Mahasu *devata* at Hanol is one of the most venerated temple of Jaunsar-Bawar region. The façade of the temple has an extensively carved wooden door frame with three arched receding door jambs. The first two inners jambs having scenes of *Ramayan* origin whereas the outer door jamb has scenes derived from *Mahabharat* and *Puranas*. Also the vertical wooden planks on either side of the arched door–way also do have panels having similar subject matter.

They depict warriors in fighting postures with bow and arrow or wrestling with their maces lying on ground beside them. One of the panels is carved with a view of Kurukshetra battle field. Here Bhishm is lying on a bed of arrows which had pierced his body. When Bhishm asked for water, Arjun is depicted with a bow in his hand, while the other pulls back the string, suggesting, that the arrow is being released, The shot by Arjun is again shown hitting the ground-causing a fountain of pure water gushing out of the earth and falling into Bhishm's mouth.

Another panel depicts Arjun in disguise of Brihnnal whispering something in the ear of Prince Uttar of Viratnagar, where the Pandav lived incognito. When Duryodhan had attacked Viratnagar, Arjun in the disguise of Brihannal offered to act as Prince Uttar's charioteer. But on seeing warriors like Bhishm, Duryodhan, Draunacharya and Karn, Uttar lost his confidence and wanted to go back. Then Arjun asked him to drive the chariot instead and decided to fight those brave warriors. The panel being discussed seems to depict the dialogue between Brihannal, and Arjuns. Another panel depicts a female with bow and arrow stretched: mounted on a chariot. This too seems to be representation of Arjun as Brihannala and the charioteer seems to be prince Uttar. In the similar panel, there is another figure in the foreground with a wheel in his raised right hand. This is Abhimanyu with the wheel of his broken chariot in his hand, whirling it above his head and rushing at the enemy. It was when he had no weapons left with him since Dronacharya's arrow had broken his sword and Karn had broken his armour. Though the two war scenes took place at different places and at different times, but the artisan engaged in the task of carving, regardless of strict adherence to historical accuracy in terms of time and space, has squeezed two episodes in one panel.

The vertical row of wooden panels on the side of the arched door frame, has two panels, showing Draupadi's *cheerharan*. The lower panel depicts Dushasan pulling Draupadi's *sari*. The upper panel depicts Kirshn with his one hand raised in *abhaya mudra* and from his other hand he is releasing endless roll of *sari* which saved the prestige of Draupadi. The factor connecting the two panels is the *sari* which emerges out of lord Krishna's hand in one panel and continues to the other lower panel where Draupadi's *sari* is being pulled off by Dushashan. The top most panel is carved with five Pandavs. One horizontal plank supporting the roof of the temple on the right side depicts Bhim pulling Jarasandh's leg to kill him. Another panel is carved with Draupadi being dragged by Dushasan. With her hand stretched towards Lord Krishna playing flute on right, she is pleading for his help.

The canopied composite roofed temple of Chalda Mahasu *devata* at Thadiyar, has exquisitely carved wooden door frame. When the author visited the site in 2002 it was under construction. At that time too, carvings on its door jambs had been completed. When revisited recently in connection with the present research work, it was observed that the wooden door frame has been painted with golden colour. The temple has a Shivling in front and a huge concrete sculpture of Nandi opposite the temple in its open courtyard in front of the temple.

The carvings on its wooden door frame repeat some scenes of *Mahabharat* derivation, viz., Dushasan pulling Draupadi holding her hand, Arjun aiming at the eye of the fish on top of a pole by looking at its reflection in the water below. Just above is probably Draupadi again with a garland in her up-raised hands for putting the garland around Arjuna's neck. The top most vertical row of the panels includes two panels, which are much similar to those depicting Draupadi's *cheerharan* at Hanol The lower panel depicts Dushasan pulling off Draupadi's *sari* and five helpless Pandavs seated in front. Her *sari* continues to the panel above, where it is emerging as an endless piece of cloth from Lord Krishna's left hand, who responded to her prayers as her Saviour. There is a *chakra* in his right upraised hand. All the above mentioned panels constitute the right portion of the wooden door frame as viewed from front. The *Mahabharat* scenes carved on the wooden panels forming part of the left side of the door frame include : Abhimanyu with a wheel of his broken chariot whirling above his head whereas Jayadrath aims at him with his stretched bow and arrow, Bhism lying on the bed of arrows whereas Arjun in the act of striking the ground with his arrow. A stream of water is seen gushing out of the earth and dropping in the month of thirsty Bhishm.

The old tower temple of Pawasi *devata* at Chinwa was in the process of being replaced by a new structure when visited. Here one new panel pertaining to *Mahabharat* origin was seen lying against a wall for fixing on the temple wall. It depicted Draupadi's *swayambar* with Arjun hitting the eye of a fish with his arrow with the help of its reflection in the water pond below.

The gable-roofed temple of Kali at Koti-Kanesar is dedicated to the Brahmanical pantheon. It also shows some episodes from *Mahabharat,* viz. Bhishm on the bed of arrows and Arjun hitting the ground with bow and arrow and a water-fountain springing out and dropping in Bhishm's mouth. In this panel Duryodhan has also been depicted in the background bringing water. Adjacent to it is depicted Duryodhan-*vadha* in another scene. The inner most door jamb shows Draupadi's *cheerharan* carved on it.

The multi-tiered pyramidal roofed temple of Basik *devata* at Kuna richly embellished with exquisite carvings on its wooden components has a mixture of scenes with thematic connotation having sources in both – the Brahamanical as well as the indigenous cult and life. The second door jamb of the door of the door of the verandah, on the right side shows Arjun holding a bow and arrow aiming at the eye of the fish above by looking at its reflection in the water pond below, to fulfill the condition kept by the king Drupad — an episode pertaining to Draupadi's *swayambar*. We find similar depiction on a wooden panel under the beam supporting the roof. The panel adjacent to it most probably depicts Dushasan dragging Draupadi.

One massive wooden pillar in the verandah show a *chakra* or wheel like form, on the left and a warrior on right with a bow and arrow who is youthful in his appearance . This seems to be depiction of *chakravyuh* and the warrior on right is Abhimanyu, who knew the art of penetrating *chakravyuh*, to attack but was skilled by the treachery of Duryodhan and Dronachary. Live performance of *chakravyuh* is a part of the cultural performances in the region and runs for about 30 to 90 days in Alaknanda, Mandakini, Pindar, and Bhagirathi valleys.

Some wood-carving seen at the pyramidal temple at Kuna, probably, seems to have symbolic reference to the events of *Mahabharat*. For example, the massive wooden pillar in the verandah shows a web-like hexagonal form and a figure at its back. A pointed covered-shell is shown in the centre. It could be the artist's presentation of *kamalvyuh* — a formation of defence in the battlefield designed by Dronachary to protect Jaydrath from Arjun who had rowed to kill him by the sword to avenge the dishonouring the deadbody of his brave son Abhimanyu on the battlefield. The hexagonal formation had another minor protective core-formation within in the pattern of *shankh* or pointed shell where Jayadrath was kept. Dronachaya knew that except Krishn no one could break this *vyuh-rachna* (complex battle formation). Knowing its invincibility Krishn planned a trick. He hailed goddess Yogmaya to help and create a screen of clouds to cover the sum and create an illusion of sunset. As this happened, Jaydrath came out of the *chakravyooh* to happily witness Arjun ending his life as per his vow. Soon the clouds disappeared as per Yogmaya's spell and Jaydrath was killed by Arjun as per his vow. The covered shell in the centre of the hexagonal cow web like form could be symbolic of the *kamal-chakravyooh*. The figure with snake could be Krishn who subdued Kalia- the serpent demon. The small figure with an arrow could represent Arjun perhaps.

The above presumption is one possibility since episodes from *Mahabharat* have been popular among the natives of this region. Boda Badhi, extraordinarily gifted carver of Kuna temple, as he was known, might have been very innovative in his symbolic representation.

Another wooden panel also shows a wheel-like form with a figure in the centre with hands stretched out without weapons. This too, possibly, seems to depict Abhimanyu trapped in *kamal-*

chakravyuh . Whether this figure could be a *Nagraj*, will be examined further under the sub-title 'Themes from *Pauranic* sources." However, the study, has revealed that episodes from *Mahabharat* involving the Pandavs and Kauravs have been very poplar in the Jaunsar-Bawar and Rawain belt of central Himalaya perhaps due to the belief of socio-historical links among the natives as noticed in their frequent repetition in the wood carvings seen at different places.

Pauranic Source

Pauranic literature has been very close to the life of the Indian layman and it influenced the mind of the people so profoundly that not even the two great epics *Ramayan* and *Mahabharath* could do.[32] *Puran* were ancient Indian compilations in Sanskrit verses pertaining to Hindu mythology. According to encyclopaedia Britannia their origin is traceable to vedic times.[33] The reference to the word *Puran* goes back from Vedic period upto the scriptures of the 11th cent. The span of creation and compilation of *Purans* is approximately between 600 BC to 700 A.D.

"They share much material with the two great epics, the Mahabharata and Ramayan (qq.v), and with the law books (dharma sastra). "Purana" means "ancient,", and traditionally , purana treats of the creation of the world, its destruction and renewal, the genealogy of gods and seers, the great ages of mankind, and the history of dynasties. However, of the 18 principal surviving puranas, the majority are of sectarian character, concerned with devotion to Siva or Visnu . . . .. They contain much devotional material (bhakti), eulogies on shrines, the duties of the castes, and descriptions of Vedic-brahmanical customs and ceremonies. Recitation and exposition of purana in temples and annually in Bhrahman households form an important aspects of Hindu devotion."[34]

There are 18 *purans*, viz. 1. *Brahma*, 2. *Vishnu*, 3. *Shiv*, 4. *Bhagvad*, 5. *Bhavishyat*, 6.*Nardiy*, 7. *Markanday*, 8. *Agni*, 9. *Brahmavaivart*, 10. *Ling*, 11. *Varaha*, 12. *Skanda*, 13. *Vaman*, 14. *Matasya*, 15. *Garud*, 16. *Brahmand*, 17. *Padh*, 18. *Kurm*.

So far as the themes of the wood work in Jaunsar-Bawar and Rawain regions are concerned, it is the generally related to genealogy of gods, more specifically the life and deeds of the gods, specially Krishn, Shiv and Vishnu, which have been popular as subject matter among the native carvers of the region.

The temple of Mahasu *devata* at Hanol is richly carved where the scenes related to episodes and deeds on the heroic life of the valorous Lord Krishn. — a popular subject matter have found manifestation. On the richly carved and gaudily painted façade of the temple-entrance — an arched wooden door frame, the upper jamb depicts scenes related to Krishn-lila (Pl. 6, 7, 9, 12, 13, 17, & 20). Among them are Lord Krishn holding the elephant Kuvaliapeed's trunk whom villainous Kans sent to kill Krishn, Krishn playing flue standing on the hood of snake Kalia nag (*Kaliyamardan*); *Cheer-haran* (stealing of the clothes of *gopis*) , wherein *gopis* forming a phalanx on the right and Krishn with their clothes on the left side are depicted; Shishupal-*Vadh*; Krishn playing flute with *gopis*; Krishn dragging Kans by his hair from his thrown on to the floor, infront; Krishn sucking Putna *rakshasi* sent by Kans (she was eventually unable to free herself from Krishn and subsequently died (Pl.....); Kans holding Yashoda's new born daughter in his hand (mistaking her to be the daughter of Devki and Vasudeva), about to hurl her against the rock while Devki stands in awe.

Among the other *pauranic* themes we come across Vasudev wading through Yamuna with his new born eighth son Krishn in a basket, Kans with Vasudev and Devki in the palace (or jail), child Krishn astride Trinavart, Kansa's attendant, who carried away child Krishn in the guise of whirlwind (here depicted in human form). When Trinvart could not bear the weight of the child Krishn he fell down in Brij and died at last. On the racking plank of the gable roof *raslila* is carved. The figures of Krishn with flute and *gopis* are alternately depicted with the hands of the latter placed on the shoulders of the former.

Besides on the horizontal panel supporting the roof, is carved *cheerharan* — Krishna playing flute beneath a tree on the left and nude *gopis* on the right with folded hands praying for the return of their clothes. River is depicted by spiraling waves. Another panel depicts Krishn on the right with his hands stretched out towards *gopis* holding butter-pots in their hands while Balram with plough is standing on left. Though traditional peacock-plume on Krishn's crown is missing but there is no doubt about the theme since the flute resting diagonally across his left leg and the butter-pots held by two maids are indicative of the episode. There is a another panel under the pent roof, which is carved within a niche in centre. In the upper half a seated figure with folded hands is flanked by two figures in similar pose on either side. The row of heads shown suggests other devotees in background. The lower half shows a cow prominently. The male figure in centre wears a crown with a peacock plume in centre. It apparently seems to depict Krishn.

Among the gods and goddesses carved on the pediment Krishn stealing butter, Gaja-Laxmi, Durga, Shiv-*tandava*, Ganesh, Hanuman with Lord Ram, Hanuman playing *manjiras*, five-headed and ten -armed Hanuman etc., can be seen. On the wooden plank on the right side of the temple, supporting the roof from which fringes are suspended. Krishn is depicted playing flute with a cow beside him. Above the cow a peacock is perched on a tree. Another scene carved here shows infant

Krishn tied with a rope with a tree, crouching on the ground. The tree is miraculously uprooted by Krishn's divine power liberating the captive souls. Some figures with folded hands are shown standing in awe. In the panel above image of Shiv has been carved. One of the panels depicts *devi* in seated posture (Pl.31). She is eighteen-armed holding attributes in each hand, viz., *dand* (stick), *darpan* (mirror), *dhanush-ban* (bow and arrow), *shankh* (conch), *ankush* (elephant's goad), *vajra* (thunderbolt), *gada* (mace), *kutthar* (axe) and *akshamala* (rosary). In her left hands from the top she holds *chakra* (disc.), *pash* (noose), *trishul*, (three pronged spear), *patra* (vessel supposedly filled with wine), *ghanta* (bell), k*hatvanga* (a club), *kunta* (small spear) K*hadag* (small knife), *tanka* (chisel).

"The *chakra* and the *gada* which are also symbols of Vishnu, when held in *Devi's* hands emphasize the Viashnav connection."[35] We find exquisite examples of eighteen-armed *Durga's* stone sculptures from medieval period. Another wooden panel depicts eleven-headed, ten-armed and eight-legged goddess of time — Kali wearing the garland of skulls and a skirt around her waist made of human arms. Her tongue hangs out signifying her ferocity. The garland of skulls symbolizes liberated souls and the human hands tied round her waist remind one to dedicate all actions to the goddess.

The above two manifestations of Durga reveal tantric aspect associated with the *shakt* sect. . One of the panels forming side wall of the pent roof of the temple also has a representation of Kali standing on a corpse. Four-armed she is holding her attributes, wearing a garland of skulls with her tongue hanging out. A wooden panel under the roof on the right side of the temple is carved with an eight-armed Durga in *asan* posture. Another wooden panel adjacent to it depicts Mahagauri, one of the Navdurgas, seated on a bull. She wears a *sari* holding her trident in right hand but in the other instead of *damru,* she has a *padma.* Besides, she has just two hands in place of four generally associated with her iconography.

Shiv is another god who had been a popular subject matter for carvings in wood in the region. Wooden plank under the roof shows Lord Shiv seated cross legged with a trident in his hand. In another panel Shiv as *Gangadhar* is seen seated cross-legged and Ganga is emerging out of the tuft over his head. His right hand holds a trident and the left one rest on an arm-rest. A *kamandal* is shown beside him. Another vertical plank forming the wall of the same pent-roof, bears a carved image of the bearded Brahma with wide open eyes, holding a *Ved* in his left hand and his right-hand is held in the *abhay mudra* . It is interesting to note that miniature wooden statues of Brahma holding the *Vedas* are fixed in the four miniature gables affixed back to back over the pent roof of the *garbhagriha* . He is shown wearing a striped shirt and a *rudraksha mala*, a dhoti with arranged parallel folds and the *Ved* in right hand. It is painted with yellow, brown, white, black and skin colours. His body is carved only upto thighs and is placed on a lotus pedestal painted with red and green colours. It is a unique and distinct example of its own type seen in this region.

There is an interesting scene carved on a panel of the wooden façade of the main entrance of the temple. Here Lord Shiv is seated cross legged with a *trishul* and *damru* in his hands on a stylized tree. The tree trunk is flanked by a demon on either side, who are engaged in cutting the tree with a saw they hold in their hands. According to the popular belief in this region the two demons in the third world — *pataklok*, are engaged in their malicious attempt to cut the tree on which the earth rests and cause the end of the world. But due to the blessings of Lord Shiv on the people of this world, they are not able to get success in their attempts. This legend having its origin in the popular beliefs of the natives of the region of Jaunsar-Bawar and Rawain has also been witnessed in wood-carvings at other centres.

The other deities carved on the door-jamb of the main entrance include, three-headed Brahma seated on a lotus, Ganesh, Vishnu and Laxmi seated on modern chairs, with Sheshnaga at the back and flanked by standing images of Saraswati in the right and another figure, probably of an attendant with a *chauri*, to the left and 'creation of Brahama.' Brahma, the first creation of this material world is depicted born on a lotus flower, sprouting from the navel of *garbhodaksayi* Vishnu. The latter is an expansion of *karanodakasayi* Vishnu, who is turn is an expansion of *Sankarsana. Sankarsana* is an expansion of Balarama, who is turn is an immediate expansion of Lord Krsihna.[36] Vishnu is seated on a stool like object with his navel cord rising up in the space, with a lotus on which Brahma's image is carved. Laxmi, is seated in front of Vishnu with her hand placed on his feet.

In the multitiered Pyramidal roof temple of Basik *devata* at Kuna excellent carvings are executed on the wooden beams, pillars, ceiling of the veranda and balcony and the wooden door jambs of the cella as well as that of the veranda's door. On the lintel of the cella door Ganesh is carved in centre, flanked by two attendants on either side (leaning backward) blowing *shankhs*. On the third jamb on the right side Mahishasurmardani is shown crushing the demon Mashissura under her feet. She holds a trident in her right hand. Below her is carved Vishnu in the incarnation of Narasimha. Further below are the other Brahminic images. Shiv astride his *vahan* Nandi (bull) is holding a trident in his right hand and on the right side is depicted his consort Parvati. The second door jamb shows Kartikey mounted on his *vahana* peacock, *Varahavatar* Vishnu, Indra mounted on his *vahana* elephant (Eravat) etc.

On the fourth door jamb on the right is an images of *Surya* holding a lotus in each hand. In sculptures too he is often depicted holding two fully expanded lotus. Just like a sunflowers, they resemble the solar disc.

The second door jamb on the left side has a male figure with his *shakti*. On the third door jamb on the left, again a male is shown with locks of hair hanging on both sides. They both probably represent Kartikey. The third door jamb on this side depicts again the image of *Surya* (sun) with lotus in both hands. Below him is *Varahavatar* of Vishnu. Another interesting scene depicted here is two *rakshasas*, seated on either side of a tree on which rests the earth, trying to cut the tree to destroy the earth but unable to do so due to benevolence of the deity (Shiv) carved above.

The sixth door jamb on the left again depicts goddess Durga and a female seated with lotus in her hands which represents *Kamaldharini* Laxmi.

The massive pillars in front of the cella and on either side of the verandas entrance are heavily carved with decorative motifs and mythological scenes. On one of the pillars six armed goddess holding *chakra, sword, trishul*, a bow and arrow etc., is depicted riding on a lion. On another pillar some mystical creatures are carved. Below them a male is carved holding snakes in his hands. Another snake is encircled on his waist. In front of him is a web like form with eight snakes emerging from the centre. Though as discussed earlier, possibly, the panels could be symbolic depiction of the events of *Mahabharat*, it is also possible that this could be related to the Mahasu cult as one of the legends mentions them as a *naga* deity.

Since, the image holds a snake in his hands and only his body upto waist is visible the (lower part is covered with a web of snakes), this could be personified representation of Nagraj. We come across similar representation at other centres also, but the web of snakes noticed here is unique. The worship of snake (*nag-pooja*) among the Hindus has been a common practice. *Nag*-image or the theme related to it is frequently depicted in relief in stone and wood also at many places.

The importance of serpents in the legends is manifested in their worship, and the *nag*-worship in India is aided by the construction of temple dedicated to them. One often finds stone slabs decorated with serpent motifs set near the water sources to ensure their blessings. Such temples are commonly small wooden structures with peaked shingled roofs open on four sides and containing within an image of the *nag* to be worshiped, such as the temple of the Karshan Nag found in Suill Valley.[37] Snakes in Indian Art are depicted with upper part of the figure of human being and the lower part of snake. The serpent is often conceived of as a three, five, seven or nine headed being.

The *nag* is a figure representing the residue that remained after the earth, the upper and infernal regions, and all their beings, had been shaped out of the cosmic waters of the abyss.

The serpent, symbolizing the life-force that motivates birth and rebirth… like a river winding its away, the serpent creeps along the ground, it dwells in the earth and start forth like a fountain from its hole. It is an embodiment of the water of the life issuing from the deep body of Mother Earth.[38] Since the serpent moves forth from the hole like a fountain there could be the possibility that this aspect of the serpent might have inspired in this particular carving on the massive wooden column, i.e. eight serpent coming forth just like a fountain.

One of the columns of the verandah is carved with a ten-headed and sixteen-armed deity, who seems to be *Devi*, as some of the identical attributes are : *panapatra, chakra, khadag, ghanta, dhanush-ban, pustak* etc. (vessel, wheel, small knife, bell, bow and arrow and manuscript respectively). Durga as Mahisasurmardini is also carved on one of the columns. The temple priest with a lamp and a bell is his hands suggest the daily ritual practiced in the temple.

The entire wooden door of the main entrance leading to the verandah of the temple at Kuna is decorated with carved images of gods and goddesses which include many from the Brahamanical source, viz. eight-armed goddess Durga riding on her *vahan*-lion, seated Lord Surya holding the long steams of disc-like lotus motif. Below it is a male seated with a small figure of female seated on his right thigh with his attribute in his left upraised hand, where as the right hand and the face of the female is hidden behind the metallic knob of the door. This figure appears to be representation of Laxmi-Narayan. Below it is carved Mahisasurmardani and in the centre of the lower part of the door is depicted goddess Saraswati seated cross legged with *veena* held diagonally across her body.

The Shiv temple at Lakhamandal has gable roofed verandah in front. It has religious and mandane figures carved on it. One of the columns is carved with the a figure of Shiv mounted on his *vahan* Nandi. Just above it are two figures carrying the palanquin of the *devata*.

The arched wooden door of the temple of Chalda Mahasu at Thadiyar also depicts scenes from Pauranic sources viz., *Kaliamardan* scene, Lord Shiv, goddess Durga mounted on her *vahan* lion, goddess Laxmi, a *nag* deity with a snake hood over his head. Yashoda behind the cradle with infant Krishn. Another scene depicts Kans holding new born daughter of Devki in his upraised hands, in a gesture of hurling it against the rock and Krishn playing flute with a cow behind him.

A noteworthy representation here is that of *Ardhanarishvar*, which symbolises perfect unison of Shiv and Shakti showing right and left part of the composite figure respectively. Parvati dons a *sari* and jewellery, whereas Shiv is shown only in a lion-cloth and a few garlands giving pale effect. According to the mythological belief when both are depicted in unison symbolizing the creative aspect of Shiv-Shakti, the latter (*Devi* as Shakti)is believed to have absorbed Shiv-*tattva* into herself and hence pale (or white) complexion.

The canopied composite roofed wooden temple at Kharsali has rich ornamentation on the wooden components of the temple. The front wall of the *mandap*, wooden ventilators on its top, door frame of the second *mandap*, the racking plank of the gable roof, all present a good quality of carvings on wood. The five females are carved on a wooden plank forming part of the front wall of the *mandap*. Facial features and clothes have been simplified, suggested through minimum details rendered in the folk style. These could be representation of *Matrikas* which usually are depicted by seven figures. Two owl like birds facing each other are perched on a branch of tree suspended in air. The hilly regions do have the tradition of depicting figures with few details, rather they preferred simplification with minimum details enough to denote the identity rather in few simplification. They were not interested in the outer realistic representation, usually with not few lines in folk style. As the study of the thematic subject-matter carved here revealed that there has not been strict adherence to the iconographical accuracy on the part of the artisans as per the content of the Brahamanical scriptures. Mixing of the pure imaginative motifs of the carver/s or images from the local folklore might have got mixed up with mythological characters or the themes, e.g. two birds shown face-to-face above the female figures (*Matrikas*). In India teracota imags of mother goddess and representation of *saptmatrikas* dates back to very early period. However and possibly, its traces survived in the native arts of the region. "the impact of new-Brahmin art was the least on the paintings associated with the cult of the mother-goddess and her various aspects."[39]

The canopied-composite roofed temple of Jamdagini *rishi* at Than has a verandah in front with four wooden columns supporting a cross beam on which are fixed smaller upper columns supporting the gable roof. The upper columns have carved figures of gods and goddesses. One of the columns is carved with the image of Balaram in high relief. He holds a mace and a plough in his hands. Another is carved with Krishn playing flute flanked by a *gopi* on either side and a peacock above them. There is an image of four–armed Mahisasurmardani carved on one wooden column crushing the demon Mahish under her feet.

In the canopied composite-roofed temple of Bhairav at Sankari the wooden deity is placed against the rear wall in the centre of the cella. Carved out of a rectangular block of wood, it is a very simplified figure with a disproportionately big head, short neck and his chest marked by an oblong circle formed by parallel arms with hands folded in front. His facial features are carved out in low relief. The figure is more like a totem. Besides, the beam resting on the pillars of the porch, carved with a row female figures with each other's hand in hand. They are carved in low relief and could be the *Matrikas* or a group-folk dance by the village bellies.

There is a canopied composite roofed Raghunath temple at Pujaili. The sprayed wooden door frame of the temple has seven jambs on either side and lintels above, each diminishing inwards in thickness. On the second door jamb on the right is depicted a seated male figure in *lalitasan*, and another smaller female figure with her foot on a pedestal. On the left corner is a mace-like object. The pair represents Laxmi-Narayan. Below is carved an elephant with a male holding a *vajra* like object and it could be the representation of Indra. The fifth door jamb on top depicts a cross-legged female figure, seated on a lotus flower holding lotuses in the two raised hands. Similar figure is also carved on one of the door jamb on the left. Below it is carved *Mahisasur-mardani*, her leg placed on the Mahisasur she is killing with a trident held diagonally across the body.

The canopied composite roofed temple of Karn at Deorah, though has various religious and decorative motifs carved in wood, very few figures of deities are noticed in carvings which are rendered in the simplified folk style. The female figures holding hand-in-hand in a row carved in low relief, could be the representation of *Matrikas*. Their typical headgear and heavily pleated skirts are in the local fashion commonly witnessed in the region.

The canopied composite roofed wooden temple of Duryodhan at Saur, now popularly called Someshwar temple, has a beautiful face image of Someshwara *devata* placed against the wall over an old wooden Beam of the cella. On it's front are carved female figures wearing *Pahari* comstume with hand-in-hand. This may be a localized version of the *Matrikas*, as noticed at other centres but it cannot be said with certainty in the absence of other specific symbolic evidence. The female figures here are shown wearing caps and short shirts — a local fashion. The possibility of these figures performing folk dance (a common phenomenon of the region) can not be ruled out. But since the beam forms the part of the interior of the cella, specifically where the face-image of the god is placed there is greater possibility of their being *Matrikas* in the indigenous costume of hills.

The door jambs of the temple of Kaun *devata* at Arakot has gods and goddesses of Pauranic origin carved on it which include Indra, six-armed Durga astride her *vahan* lion, Krishn playing flute, Ganesh etc.

The tower type temple of Pawasi *devata* at Chinwa was also visited by the author earlier in 2002. When the original old structure of darkened wood showing its antiquity was its too apparent feature with carved panels showing a distinctively very unique style of exquisite carving. When the temple was revisited by the author in 2011, to my great surprise, the old structure had been demolished and the fine antique wood-work was either burnt as fuel or destroyed due to the ignorance of the villagers about its historical and artistic value as well the lack of interest of the official machinery or any policy about the preservation of the valuable cultural heritage of this state in the rural interior of the region. Specimens of the old wood work seen-earlier have also been considered to prove the Brahamanical influences as well for their throwing light on the changes taking place in terms of their quality, subject matter and style as compared to the recent work witnessed in the new structure of the temple under construction.

The old tower temple at Chinwa was unique not only for its antiquity and design but also for the richly décorated wooden surface with fine specimens of sculpture in relief. The craftsman had hardly left any exposed wooden surface of the structure without manifestation of his creative skill and fertile imagination. The door - frame, exterior of the wooden beams and planks on the roof-edges, railing of the balcony, all were profusely decorated with imaginatively carved themes and motifs, wooden fringes and rosettes suspended from the roof-extremities like frill on a bride's costume. They not only display the artistic skill of the craftsman who executed them but also his devotion and innovative use of mythology, local legends, and life and environment around him.

The balcony of the temple above the entrance had eight thematic panels on the front and two on its right side. The balcony on the right side has twenty one panels. All through the length of the balcony the panels in relief were alternated by two slender columns. Each of the wooden panel had been carved in sunk-relief technique so as to leave flat frame on its surface with the desired figures within in low relief. The carved out surface of the panel, though generally rectangular in shape, did not observe uniformity in all the panels. The artist had used his discretion to use the carved space as per the shape and design of the motifs.

The themes depicted predominantly were derived from the Hindu mythology. Figures of Ganesh, Shiv, Krishn playing flute, Brahma with lotus, *Devi* seated on a lion, Balram, other gods or *ganas* with bows and arrows in cambat poses could be prominently seen. Besides some figures like a snake with human head (*nag-raja*) a man blowing – *ranasingha* (a long turret), *rakshas* cutting the earth-tree held over the back of another *yaksha*, multi-headed male figure etc. could be based on local legends.

The wooden plans underneath the balcony and the roof also showed different themes carved on their exterior. They had been executed in a frieze-like manner depicting rows of the equestrian warriors, *matrikas* and other decorative motifs.

The wooden door frame composed of four Jambs on either side, each raised outward over the other's surface with equal numbers wooden lintels was also decorated with mythololgical subjects in low reliefs. They were partly worn out and damaged.

Vishnu holding lotus and *ayudhs* in his hands, Kartikay with *shakti* in his hand , *Varahavatara*, Draupoadi-*swayambar* a male holding snakes in both hands and many snakes surrounding him, six-armed goddess etc., many mythological subjects were depicted on the jambs and lintels of the main entrance. *Matrikas*, intertwined snakes, hanuman figures in series were depicted on the lintels.

The ceiling of the porch also had rectangular panels measuring about 12"x18" with figures carved on them. Having turned black they were hardly noticeable but show good craftsmanship.

The wooden door frame of the adjacent temple of god's *bir* also is decorated with similar subject carved on them, specially the warriors with bows and arrows, or swords and shields, are noticeable. Numerous coins, also witnessed on the main temple door, can be also seen nailed on its door and frame as offerings by the villages.

When the temple of Pawasi *devata* was revisited in 2011, only two old wooden panels carved with pauranic deities were found lying under the porch. One of these is divided into two parts by a decorative strip shows *Varhavatar* Vishnu with *padma* (lotus) and a *chakra* (wheel) in hands, standing in front view with the head of a boar in profile view. He is flanked by a fish on either side below.

Vishnu in *Varahavatar* saved the planet earth which had been submerged into the cosmic ocean by the demons. The helpless *devas* or gods prayed Lord Vishnu to save the earth. So he assumed the form of a splendid, gigantic boar and dived into the cosmic ocean and lifted the earth with his tusks out of the waters. The two fish carved on either side of *Varhavatar* standing on the back of Garud, his vehicle Varha avatar are symbolic of water of the ocean.

Another old panel found lying under the porch was that of eleven headed and twenty-armed. Ravan holding different arms in each hand, apparently the chief villian of *Ramayan*.

The rectangular door-frame of the temple of Pawasi *devata* under construction at Chinwa has four arched door frames. The entire wooden frame has been exquisitely carved with elaborate depiction of a variety of episodes derived from the epics. The scenes carved on the door jambs pertaining to Pauranic sources include – Shiv *Ling* with two devotees on either side pouring water on it, seated image of Lord Shiv, Brahma seated on a lotus with one hand raised in *abhaya-mudra*, two-armed Vishnu with a lotus and a mace, Shesha-shai Vishnu reclining (on the *sheshanag* with Laxmi seated in front). Skand also known as Kartikey and Kumar, the son of Shiv, and Parvati, mounted on his *vahan* peacock and Vishnu as Varahavatar with earth resting on his tusks. When revisited the temple, the veteran craftsman Gangaram, was engaged in carving images of gods and goddesses in high relief on wooden blocks. Among them we could see Durga, Krishn, Shiv, Ganesh and Hanuman.

Two wooden panels forming the part of the first door jamb on the left, together showed an interesting episode related to the birth of Brahma. One panel depicts Sheshashai Vishnu reclining on Adishesh with his leg stretched straight and placed on the lap of Laxmi as she presses his feet. The front portion shows spiralically arranged coils of Sheshnag, whose hood serves as a parasol over Vishnu.

In another panel, from Vishnu's navel emanates the original fully bloomed lotus. (carved in the other panel above) with Brahma seated with folded hands in veneration. The is unique device to solve the limitation of space by joining two panels for one episodes which reflects the artist's ingenuity.

The façade of the gable roofed wooden temple of Mahasu *devata* at Zadi has large wooden panels carved with the images of Vishnu, Brahama, Shiv, Krishn playing flute, Radha and Krishn, Durga, Saraswati, Kali carved on it. They bear remembrance to the contemporary calendar art. The original or older wooden panels with carvings done on them show a very primordial folk style, though some Pauranic deties are carved in low relief, viz., Shiv and Durga.

The temple of Kali at Koti Kanesar has a wooden door-frame with a carvings executed on it in low relief, depicting gods and goddesses of Pauranic origin. The entrance door of the temple is carved with heavy bodied figure of goddess Kali who has a broad and long face, with wide open eyes and the tongue hanging out of the mouth.

The four armed goddess wears a garland of human heads symbolizing liberated souls. Human arms tied to her waist remind us to dedicate all actions to the goddess Kali. She stands on the body of Shiv. As per a legend Shiv did so to stop her from the undisturbed wrath and destruction. Another scene on the door-jamb on the left shows Vasudeva wading though the river Yamuna with new born Krishn in the basket on his head. The latter is being sheltered from rain by Sheshanag. The other carvings on right door Jamb depicts the birth of Brahma, Shiv, Krishna playing flute, Ganesh and Laxmi-Ganesh are also carved on the other panels of the door jambs.

Apparently, the fact that most of the traditional temples in the villages are originally dedicated to the native deities (Mahasu), the traces of the cultural links to Brahmanism and Hindu mythology continued to survive in the ethos of the natives and gradually got manifestation in the carvings of wood craft, as well as identifying the classical heroes with the local deities by dedicating some wooden temples to characters from *Mahabharat* and the mixing up of the concepts and the cults of Mahasu and *Maha-Shiv* in the region. The trend clearly establish the increasing influences in the original cult and wood carvings of Brahaminism.

There is a temple of Mahasu *devata* at Lakhwar. The present structure has been recently built replacing the original temple. The temple has two floors. The ground floor comprises of a huge hall which has a balcony on three sides. The front side of the balcony opens into a semi-circular porch on the second floor is an assembly hall in the centre flanked by twin cellas of Mahasu *devata* on the right and that of Chalda Mahasu on the left. The wooden door frames and doors of the edifice are very intricately and exquisitely carved with figures of gods and goddesses of *Pauranic* origin. The arched door jamb of the temple of Chalda Mahasu is carved with the images from the Brahmanical pantheon — Laxmi, Saraswati, Shiv, four-armed Durga astride her *vahan* lion, Shiv, with his *vahan* Nandi (bull), Laxmi–Narayan, Laxmi-Ganesh, Krishna playing flute etc. The wooden door of the temple has standing images of lord Shiv, Ganesh, *astabhuja* Durga mounted on her *vahan* lion etc. The deities are executed with great refinement, perfection, delicacy and naturalism, making it an outstanding religious edifice in this region but lacking the native fervor.

Within the two cellas of Mahasu *devata* on the extremes of a small assembly hall the marble sculptures of the respective *devatas* are placed. The arched wooden of door frame of the assembly hall shows mainly horal and floral and faunal motifs carved on it with few exceptions of the images of Hindu gods like Krishna playing flute. The most outstanding carvings, so far witnessed are the deities of Pauranic origin on the wooden door frame and the door of the assembly hall on the first floor. The central panel of this arched door frame is carved with

Navdurgas flanked by the image of Durga on either side. In *Devi Mahatamyam* and the *Veraha Puran* they are mentioned in the following older ; 1. Shailputri, 2. Brahamacharini, 3. Chandraghanta, 4. Kushmanda, 5. Skandamata, 6. Katyayni, 7. Kalratri, 8. Mahagauri and 9. Siddhidayani . But the carvings under discussion are depicted differently in following order : (from the left) 1. Shailputri, 2. Kushmanda, 3. Mahaguri, 4. Chandraghanta, 5. Skandamata, 6. Katyayni, 7. Kalratri, 8. Mahagauri, 9. Brahmacharini. Non adherence of the icographical order could be the artisan's ignorance.

It won't be exaggeration to say that there is hardly any wooden component at the temple of Mahasu devata at Lakhwar which is not very intricately carved. The temple is an unique example of carving in wood executed with great refinement and contemporary style perfection.

An overview of all the aforementioned centres reveal that the episodes pertaining to the life of the Pauranic gods and goddess, their different incarnations have found profuse manifestation revealing the popularity and veneration they received in these regions since ancient times.

SYMBOLS AND MOTIFS

Indian art had been heavily symbolic in nature right from the ancient times. "One need not be fluent in the language of post-structuralism to sense that the problem of symbol is merely the problem of interpretation writ large and in boldface. But the problem of symbol and symbolism strikes at the very core of much of what, we are tempted to say, is important about aesthetics and art history itself. With art so frequently taken to be a form of expression, one wants to inquire into the nature of that which is expressed and its interpretation."[40]

The art of wood carving in Garhwal Himalaya is replete with profuse use of religious symbols, which connote and convey the underlying sense or meaning in a previous manner. "A symbol "stands for" in some establishable way that which it symbolizes. A symbol serves to transfer someone's thought to something other than itself and the transfer is not a random association. The transfer depends upon certain features of the symbol which give it a place in a certain meaning system....In general, it takes both formal devices and a thing with appropriate characteristics to establish that thing or make it function as a symbol... Symbols are context dependent."[41]

Apart from the pertinence in term of interpretation of the meaning connoted by the symbols, the latter are also significant from the view point of aesthetic value they posses depending on the novelty and creativity in their treatment and ability to evolve them further by the artisans. The wood carving of the region reveals employment of great variety of symbols and motifs impregnate with meaning having roots in the religion and, hence are perhaps, considered auspicious and omnipresent throughout the state, even finding place on the front of the houses.

A human head surrounded by concentric series of flower-petals within one or more concentric circles is a common sight almost in all the temples. It symbolizes sun god. Sun is a *Vedic* god believed to be the source of life and light both responsible for causing rain (source of water) and yielding good crop. In the rural areas, specially the interior of the Himalaya. It assumes special significance. It is represented in wood carving in most of the temples. We have seen them specially in the temples at Hanol, Devalsari, Deorah, Thadiyar, Kuna etc.

The old temple of Pawasi *devata* at Chinwa, which has now been demolished to be replaced by a new structure had this motif engraved on the main door frame as well as on the main beam projecting close to the ventilator. A panel on the wooden balcony on the right side shows a superior craftsmanship. The face of the god within the circle with wide open eyes and mustaches bore smile on the lips. The lotus petals in the two concentric circles were carved in a sunk technique, i.e., showing the carved depth of each petal with its tip raised. Its craftsmanship was superior and was a unique examples of Sun god of this type seen anywhere in the wooden temple of this region.

In the temples of south India too we find examples of *Surya* (Sun) depicted with a male head surrounded by rows of lotus petals arranged within the concentric circles.[42] Another variation of the sun motifs is when depicted with whirling lines radiating from its centre [43].

The motif of sun symbol, as observed in the wood carvings of Rawai region, was further evolved by the local artisans, leading to variation in its depiction. A wooden panel at the temple of Basika *devata* at Kuna shows four concentric circles with the head of the Sun god in centre. He has a chubby face with wide open eyes touching the contours of his face, sharp projecting nose and a pointed chin. The first concentric circle consists of dots, the second one has radiating lines, the third one has tiny squares and the fourth consists of triangles . It has greater aesthetic appeal and has been carved with noteworthy refinement.

A noteworthy symbol of god *Surya* is carved on the wooden door of the entrance leading to the verandah of the temple at Kuna. It has a human head in the centre with concentric circles similar to the one discussed above. From the outer circle are emanating five heads of horses, three on left and two on right, whereas at the bottom of the circle two horses are carved with their backs at the centre. It is a unique symbol for the sun god, *Surya*, evolved by the indigenous craftsmen and it bears testimony to their creativity and novelty on his part.

Another auspicious motif seen in the wooden temples is *swastika*. It symbolizes good fortune and Vishnu, indicating four fold pattern of creation. It is also associated with snake worship since the spectacle marks on the cobra's hood are regarded as half *swastika*. The cella-door of the Mahasu temple at Kaurava for example, shows a *swastika* carved on it.

Purnghat is a symbol of over flowing prosperity, blessings and fullness of life.[45] A good example of this is found on the cella door- jamb of the temple of Karn *devata* at Deorah. A design on the ceiling of the temple of Karn at Deorah depicts a geometrical pattern with three squares set diagonally one within the other in receding order of sizes. The empty triangular space thus left is filled with floral motifs. Close to it is also as square with another diagonally set within it. The corners are filled with parallel angular lines carved on it. The centre is occupied by an open lotus "It symbolizes life floating on the surface of primordial waters. An open lotus symbolises the sun. It is a flower of life blossoming on earth. It is the visible sign of consciousness in matter."[46]

Sometimes a *trishul* (trident) is depicted independently. On the door jamb of the Raghunath temple at Pujaili a *trishul* is carved. *Trishul* is usually held by Shiv as one of the *ayudhs* and is believed to destroy the evil and impart fearlessness.

A motif which is depicted universally in wood carvings in religious edifices of this region is the snake. The areas near water springs and rivulets in the hills abound in snakes. Water springs are considered as abode of snakes. The hill people living in wild surroundings are always haunted by the fear of the awesome creature. Therefore, perhaps, in mountainous region, the practice of *nag* – worship grew over the ages, so as to propitiate it seeking protection and well being. They are depicted singly or are often entwined. When entwined they symbolize the principle of creation. We have seen examples of entwined snakes in the Raghunath temple at Pujaili. Someshwar Mahadev temple at Kharsali, temple of Karn at Deorah Mahasu temple at Hanol, temple of Bhairav at Sankari and temple of Duryodhan at Saur. Rather hardly any temple is there without snake image in some form. When snakes are held by a male in his hands, it represents the personification of the *Nag devata* which can be seen on the door lintel of the temple of Karn at Deorah. One of the door jambs of the Raghunath temple at Pujaili depicts a snake ending in a human head. It is flanked by snakes on either side. It also manifests the *Nag devata.* A panel on the railing of the balcony of the Pawasi *devata* temple at Chinwa, which has now been demolished, was also carved with the figure of the snake with torso of man. Another panel depicted a man holding snakes in hands. They both represented *Nag devata.* At Kuna too we witness such images.

Besides a variety of floral motifs dominates the decoration done in these temples both in wood as well as in embossed metal. There is no limit to the imaginativeness shown by the craftsman in creating a variety of forms and their combinations singly or in a series or group. They give the surface unique beauty as well as a feeling of vibration by its richful use for embellishment. Special mention may be made of the tree motif used in a decorative folk style to fill up the empty space. It could be few stalks with single leaf at their head sprouting from a point with a bird perched on its top or a straight stem with almost angular parallel lines shooting out from it on both sides – perhaps a symbolic representation of deodar tree. It seemed alright with the craftsman whether he used the motif vertically (the natural position) or horizontally so long as it served the basic purpose – to decorate.

Use of fish as a motif witnessed in the wooden temples of Uttaranchal has more symbolical implications that just as a creature of water. Though we have seen fish signifying water in some thematic panels (e.g. Krishn on a leaf floating on water at Hanol on the *bhandar* door, in embossed metal) but it is also represented sometimes, independently. Fish is considered as a symbol of female fertility in Pahari folk art.[47] Carved on wooden doors of the temples, the fish may symbolize here also female fertility. At the same time mountainous area with rivers flowing in the valleys and fish as a familiar and popular creature with the native artisans, it also found representation in the embellishment in wood and metal in these temples. A male when depicted surrounded by fish or holding fish in his hands could represent water deity.

WOOD CARVING IN RESIDENTIAL ARCHITECTURE

In the wake of modernization and comparatively cheap economy demanded by the houses built of concrete, stone and bricks, the wooden houses in the hills, in the course of renovation, are being replaced by the former type of building material. I was told by a local at Arakot in 2011 that the village had a big wooden residential building but now it has been replaced by a house built of stone and bricks. During my visit to the hilly region of the Garhwal Himalaya, I found that some traces of wooden residential structures could be seen.

Lakhwar village, in this context, projects some quintessential examples of wood work in residential architecture. The bunches of corn cobs hanging from ropes outside the houses with wooden components often painted brown, green and white add richness to the colourful aura of the village. Wood is employed in the construction of the gable roofs of the houses, doors, door jambs, floors, façade of the balconies, pillars.

In comparison to the wood work found in the temples, the wood work of the residences is usually simple or has decorative floral patterns and motifs. This is mainly because of the difference in the requirement and suitability based on the residential and non-residential or religious architecture. The story telling which has ever since the ages formed an essential aspect to propagate religion, has been the chief factor for the rich wood work which forms the prominent feature of the temples located in remote areas of the Garhwal Himalaya.

The residences in Lakhwar usually have sturdy door frames with receding door jambs, painted with brown, white and green colours. One door jamb of the door frame belonging to a house is carved with floral scroll. Similar floral scrolls are also carved on the planks supporting the roofs. An interesting feature is the decorative pattern and floral motif carved on the interlocking wooden beams projecting out of the door frame. The balcony, railing, pillars, roof and floor of this house are exclusively made of wood. The pillars of the railing are hexagonal and taper upwards, topped by intricately carved capitals. The first floor of the house exclusively built of wood has a pleasant and interesting interior with low roof. The wooden walls of the house have small windows pierced trough them. A peculiar feature seen in a house here was a small wooden niche type component on its exterior wall for the honey bees to make honey combs with the purpose to collect honey. A wooden plank forming a part of exterior of the wall of the house has two beautiful *munal* carved on it in indigenous style.

The use of wooden utensils must have been in vogue in the hilly regions ever since. In Lakhwar the practice of using *hukkas* with wooden parts, wooden churn-staffs holders, carved with exquisite decorative motifs still persists. Wooden boxes are still used in the Garhwal Himalayas.

On way to Karn temple, Deorah, the author came across a gable roofed composed, three storied residence. Intricately carved floral motifs on its wooden railing with pseudo slender and delicate columns forming part of it, slender tapering wooden columns of the wooden balcony projecting on the first and the third floor of this house make it a unique example of indigenous residential architecture of the Garhwal Himalaya.

At Lakhamandal we come across beautiful residential architecture. Wooden balconies of houses are carved with geometric floral motifs. Capitals of the pillars are also carved with stylized geometric floral motifs. The detail of a railing shows rhythmically treated and exquisitely carved floral scroll, flowing with great sway as if infused with sap of life. The refinement seen here is exemplary and extra-ordinary. A detail shows Garuda or *munal* like creature carved on it.

Houses at Dharali in Uttarkashi also have wooden components. Often these are simple but some lattice like designs have been witnessed in the wooden railing of the balconies.

Dehra Dun also had many old *havelis* with wooden doors, balconies, niches and wooden beams forming an essential part of the residential architecture. Unfortunately, these have been demolished and new residential and commercial buildings have taken their place. An old *haveli* has been recently demolished in Dehra Dun. This *haveli* had a sturdy wooden door and door jambs. The lintel of the door jamb has an image of Ganesh carved on it as an auspicious sign flanked by stylized floral motifs carved with great refinement and delicacy. The door jambs are exclusively carved with rhythmically flowing floral scrolls.

Unfortunately, the traditional legacy of wood work which formed an intrinsic feature of the cultural heritage of the

Garhwal Himalaya, is confronted with the danger of being lost in the wake of modernization. The indigenous people need to be made aware of its significance and serious attempts by government and non-government organizations need to taken in order to preserve it for the posterity.

References

1. Walton, H.G. Gazetteer of Dehradun (Natraj Publishers, Dehradun, 1995) pp.91-94.
2. Wikipedia, the Free Encyclopedia on ,'Historical Vedic Religion' (available on Internet). Its source is *Encyclopedia Britannica.*
3. Walton, *Op.Cit.*, (1989) p. 56.
4. *Ibid.*
5. Atkinson, *The Himalayan Gazetteer,* Vol. I, Part-II, (the Cosmo Publication, Delhi, 1973) p. 776.
6. Sharma, D.D. *Cultural History of Uttarakhand* (Indira Gandhi National Centre for the Arts), New Delhi, 2009) p. 72.
7. *Ibid.,* 81.
8. *Ibid.*
9. Dabral, Shivaprasad 'Charan,' *Uttarakhand Ka Itihas*, Part-III (Virgatha Prakashan, Dugadda, Garhwal)] p. 55.
10. Handa, O.C. *Temple Architecture of Western Himalayas : Wooden Temples* (Indus Publishing Company, New Delhi, 2001). p. 76.
11. Jain, Madhu, *The Abode of Mahashiva; Cults and Symbology in Jaunsar-Bawar in the Mid-Himalayas* (Indus Publishing Co., New Delhi, 1995) pp. 65-67.
12. Madhu Jain quotes the story as told by the priest of the temple.
13. The legend was first recorded by Hamilton and reproduced by Walton, *Op.Cit.* (1995) pp. 93-94.
14. *Ibid,* pp. 91-92.
15. Handa, *Op.Cit.* (2001) p. 75.
16. *Ibid,* p. 74.

17. Jain, *Op.Cit.* p. 64.
18. N. P. Joshi mentions to the first appearance of a snake with a Shiv image in c.6th century A.D. See Joshi, N.P. *Bhartiy Murti Vigyan* (Hindi), (Bihar Rashtra-Bhasha Parishad, Patna) p. 44.
19. Walton, *Op.Cit.*, (1989) p. 56.
20. *Encyclopaedia Britannica,* Vol. II, (1969) p. 508.
21. *Srimad Valmikiya Ramayan* (Geeta Press, Gorakhpur) Part-I, p. 117.
22. *Ibid.*

    The Ganga is knows as *Tripathga* since it purifies three paths through which it flows, i.e. the sky, the earth and the underworld (*akash, prithvi* and *patal*).
23. Sharma, D.D. *Op.Cit,* (2009) p. 44.
24. Goswami Tulsidas, *Shri Ramcharitmanas* (Geeta Press, Gorakhpur, 51st republication No. 2063), P. 687 (similar reference to Mandodari pleading Ravan to reconcile with Lord Ram also occurs on pp. 12 & 719.
25. *Valmiki Ramayan*, Part II, (Geeta Press, Gorakhpur) p. 1399.
26. For the study of wooden temple architecture of Uttarakhand refer Kamboj, *Op.Cit* (2010).
27. Sharma, *Op.Cit.* p. 44.
28. *Ibid.* pp. 44-45.
29. Purohit, D.R., "The Sacred Landscape of Pandavas : Garhwal Himalaya" in *Jaya Utsav : Celebrating Living Traditions of Mahabharat,* (Indira Gandhi National Centre for the Arts, N. Delhi, 2011). p. 85.
30. *Ibid.*
31. Ohri, Lokesh, 'Multiple Realities, Real politik and Anti Heroes : Duryodhana, and Karna of the Himalayas in a Secularizing India' in *Jaya Utsav, Op.Cit.*, p. 89.
32. Shastri, Satyacharya Jitendra Chandra Bhartiya, Sanskrit *Sahitya Ka Saral Subodh Itihas* (Hindi), (Uttar Pradesh Hindi Granth Academy, Lucknow,1977) p. 73.
33. *Encyclopaedia Britannica* (Vol. 18) p. 875.

34. *Ibid.*
35. Parthasarthy, V.R. & Parthasarthy, Indu Devi, *Goddess in Indian Art & Literature* (Bhartiya Kala Prakashan, Delhi, 2009) p. 9.
36. Prabhupada, A.C. Bhaktivedanta Swami, *Kr.s.na, The Supreme Personality of Godhead,* Vol. III (Bhaktivedanta Book Trust, Japan, 1974) p. 54.
37. Duran, Jane, 'The Nagraja: Symbol and Symbolism in Hindu Art and Iconography', in, *Journal of Aesthetic Education,* Vol. 24, No.2 (Summer, 1990) p. 41.
38. *Ibid*, Duran's Source is Heinrich Zimmer, *Myth's and Symbols,* p. 62, 67, 69 and 74.
39. Handa, O.C. *Pahari Folk Art* (Taraporevala, Bombay, 1975) p. 19.
40. Duran, *Op.Cit.,* p. 37.
41. *Ibid,* p. 38, Duran's Source is Dickie, *Aesthetics,* pp. 124-127.
42. Mitchell, *Hindu Gods and Goddesses* (Nutech Photo Lithographers, Delhi, 2001) See plate 1.
43. Jain, *Op.Cit.* p. 39.
44. *Ibid*, pp. 141-142.
45. *Ibid*, pp. 171-173.
46. *Ibid*, p. 154.
47. Handa, *Op.Cit.* (1975) p. 48.

5

Critical Appraisal

Wood carving of Garhwal Himalaya manifests a true glimpse, prolix scenario and ethos of the enchanting, sonorous, and rich religio-cultural tradition and heritage of this belt of the Central Himalaya. They evince lucrative and pervious panorama and bear testimony to the exquisite craftsmanship and skill of the virtuoso indigenous artisans of this region. Glimpses of wood carvings of Garhwal Himalaya region betray capability of the local craftsmen of producing the most original art of their own inspite of their dwellings being in the remote rural areas in the hills, and that too without any facility of a formal education or training for improvement of their skill despite the fact, that the people of this region, virtually, by and large, remained cut off from the modern developments of the plains until recent years due to the difficult terrain of central Himalaya. However, at the same time this factor, on the other hands, proved a boon for its art and had been responsible for its retaining the indigenous elements and originality of their art work. Nevertheless, due to better connectivity of the remote areas of the hills with the towns in the plain, alien and modern elements have been creeping in and penetrating in the socio-cultural fabric of the people, leaving their imprints on the wood carvings also forming part of the socio-religious edifices built during the earlier and recent past or renovated due to the damage to the wooden structure by natural factors. An extensive study of these wood carvings had been undertaken which revealed the impact of classical tradition apparently perceptible in the native art of wood carving. At many centres purely folk elements of art had been observed. Noteworthy are those sites where these two strains, or at times modern impact and as well as, simultaneously, very tribal and folk-strains, have been observed.

Thematically the Hindu mythology seems to have provided the main source, specially the two great epics- *Ramayan, Mahabharata*, and the *Bhagwat Puran*. Besides, the Pauranic gods and goddesses also provide a popular major subject-matter for the wood carvings. In order to analyse and appreciate the varied influences which have left their impact on these wood carving forming part of the socio-religio-edifices, the observations have been considered under three categories, viz., 1. The classical strains, 2. The Folk-Tribal types and 3. Other elements.

CLASSICAL STRAINS

Classical strains in the wood carvings of the Jaunsar-Bawar and Rawain regions of the Garhwal Himalaya are vividly visible in the treatment of Pauranic-deities and in the episodes taken from great epics. At Kuna, the classical impact is traceable in the figures of goddesses *Mahisasurmardaini, Saraswati* and gods carved on the wooden door of the entrance to verandah. Of special interest is Ganesh with the devotees blowing shells, flanking the former, on the lintel of the cella's door. Standing with one leg placed forward and the other drawn back, with their fully stretched bodies backward as they blow shells with their full strength, their poses render a dynamic quality to an otherwise symmetrical composition. Nowhere else do we come across such a realistic representation of the figures in profile. The roundness of limbs, their pot-bellied waist, realistic postures and gestures, all make them full of life.

The faces are generally round with plumpy cheeks, round thin realistic eyes, small lips and blunt nose. The figures carved on the door jambs and the lintels, though vary in size, poses, and dresses, seem to have some semblance and betray a single man's hand in their execution. Also on the large square wooden pillars in the verandah of the temple we notice similar treatment of the figures. They may be credited to Bona Badi, the carpenter, who is believed to have done all the work single handed as per the legend. Yet we also notice that all the figures carved here are not equally refined. It may be that some helpers also worked on the wooden reliefs in this temple.

The temple of Mahasu *devata* at Hanol has strong classical impact on its wood carvings. An interesting wood carving in this regard is the one where Vasudev is wading through the waters of Yamuna with infant Krishn in the basket. Realism in the treatment of waves, attempt to depict linear perspective, architectural details, three- dimensionality etc., are noteworthy. The figures usually are shown wearing *dhotis* tied to their waists. Actually the old tradition strengthened by conventionality since the Gupta period, might have played its role through its strains persisting in all the later art forms through medieval period. During the Gupta period classical art "became a conscious vehicle for representing religious ideas and iconography became conventionalized. "….The expressive language of hand gestures developed to perfection and the *abhay* and *varada mudra* (suggesting assurance and benevolence) were seen in many icons. The *bhanga* or flexion was introduced into the body to infuse it with grace. Postures and *asans* (sittings poses) assumed their own meaning and thus evolved the language of Indian Art."[1] Depiction of the folds of *dhoti* or *saree* by minimum folds and iconographical details do reveal an indirect classical impact of Gupta period which got evolved in the art of later Gupta period and in the early medieval period. As strains seem to have persisted through tradition with traces witnessed in the wood carvings at Thadiyar and Chinwa.

Carving of images in wood has been an age old tradition in India. Handa discovered a wooden image in July 1989 in the heap of debris lying at the back of the altar in the sanctum of Markula *Devi* at Udaipur in Lahul & Spiti district. On the wooden pillars carved with the images of Kartikey and Krishn playing flute at Than do reflect impact of later Gupta period art. The sculptural wealth seen in the niches on a wall outside on the right side of the temple bears testimony to the fact that a Nagara style temple must have existed here earlier belonging to late Gupta or early medieval period. Thus the wood carvings also do reflect the impact of the stone sculptures of the earlier period on it. The wooden door jambs of the temple at Pujaili renewal strong classical impact on the deities carved on it. The small gable roofed edifice (*kuthar*) near the temple building, beautifully carved with floral scrolls, lotus petals forming its capitals, considered auspicious in Indian art and religion, also reveal classical strains (Pl.109). In the above cited examples forms are modeled by inner pliability. Inspite of the solidity of the medium on which figures are carved the artistic transformation by the craftsmen is marked by fluid aspect, a typical classical strain. Refinement and elegance also mark the wood carvings of the above cited centres.

The Pauranic gods and goddesses carved on the wooden components of the temple at Lakhwar also reveal classical strains but they were not carved by local craftsman on the other hand, those carved wooden components more in the classical style were imported from Saharanpur.

THE FOLK- TRIBAL TYPE

A deep insight and thorough analysis of the wood carvings executed on different components of the edifices reveal the connatural folk element which at times is present in its pure form at some sites and also at places where the religious edifice is partly renovated leaving some older wooden components intact in their place. We encounter co-existence of folk, tribal and classical and sometime. modern strains simultaneously as revealed by the repertoire of wood carvings forming part of the different wooden components of the temple of Mahasu *devata* at Zadi.

The temple of Basik *devata* at Kuna also reflect folk element in its wood work. It is far more visible in the treatment of space, in the arrangement of figures and forms in a given space of a panel or wooden component, where no concern for realism, depth, perspective, anatomy of the body or nature in its natural form is discernable . Here limbs have been treated like a tube or flexible stem of a plant, and the body can take desirable twist or turn as per availability of space restricted by the limitation imposed by the shapes and sizes of the wooden components. The detail of a tree poses an interesting case study in this regard. The tree has been stylistically treated and its long leaves are more decorative than natural. On the top most leaves birds are perched adding liveliness to the view, a feature often witnessed in the folk art elsewhere in India too.

Folk element is visible at Kuna in the drapery or costume worn by some figures. They wear a piece of cloth tied to their waist, which hangs in the centre, usually having geometrical patterns carved on them. Very often the wooden beams are carved with scenes of procession, or row of warriors with weapons in their hands. Their upper body being bare, sometimes even a small dagger is fastened to the waist with a rope and usually figures are shown bare feet. Even the male are depicted wearing ear rings. These carvings reveal tribal life of those who had been inhabiting the innermost regions in this area. Folk element is also visible in the hair-do which flows like fountain on either side of the head. Specially interesting to note are the male palanquin bearers in movement, who display very lively rhythm in action as they walk. Figures are carved with naturalism showing good understanding of human anatomy and keen observation of movement. Though they wear tribal type of dress with strange hairdo suggested by parallel lines. Yet they are lively.

Folk or tribal element is also noticed in one of the two old panels found lying at the temple site at Chinwa, where construction of the new temple was undergoing. The panel is carved with eighteen-armed goddess Durga, who can be identified due to the lion on the top right corner and also from her attributes. Interestingly enough she does not wear the costume of a female and strangely is eleven-headed. The additional heads and hands symbolize the strength and great power she possess. Her lower garment fastened at the waist leaves her legs bare. Also her upper body is bare except V-shaped row of punch marks, though she wears bangles on her wrist. Her dress is very tribal in appearance and the way the lion is carved on the upper right corner with his tail encircling the entire body of the goddess is a very innovative naïve devices.

Noteworthy are the discovery of a wooden folk image of Bhairav found lying outside in the grilled and locked verandah of a store under the custody of Archeological Survey of India at the precincts of the temple at Hanol. He has a long oval face, long nose, long ear- lobes. His face is partially damaged, and his one leg and arms are missing. Though no iconographical detail is discernible due to the damage it has undergone but nearby the statue lies a small folk type image of a dog. This gives strength to the hypothesis that the wooden image at Hanol could be of Bhairav.

Both the images have folk element. Besides, there are god heads carved in high relief at Sankari and Duryodhan temple, Saur. In every wooden temple unimstakenly there had been a practice of fixing free-standing goat and mural images on the *kurad* of the temples. These were seen by the author on the kurad at Duryodhan temple-Saur Raghunath temple, Pujaili, Rudreshwar Mahadev Temple, Devalsari. At Hanol, under one of the *chhatras* there are wooden goat images fixed back to back forming its supporting column. Besides wooden images of Monal placed on *kurad* are also noticed. At some places images of snarling lion were placed at the entrance of verandah of the temple, as for example, at Devalsari and Sankari. These animal images are treated in an indigenous local folk style. Lion as the *vahan* of goddess Durga destroys the demons and *rakshashas*, and keeps the evil spirits away. Goat is sacrificed at the temples in the hills and considered auspicious. Hence goat heads are so commonly found carved in high relief or in round as noticed in these temples. A goat is also sacrificed at the time of placing of *kurad* on the temple roof.

Wood carvings at Sankari, Zadi, Netwar, Lakhamndal, Saur, Kharsali, Koti-Kanesar and Deorah reveal presence of folk elements especially in the treatment of figures and flora and fauna. The temple of Mahasu *devata* at Zadi has some of its wood carvings of gods and goddesses which are very much in folk style, highly simplified and primordial in approach. Here on a wooden panel images of Shiva and Hanuman are carved in low relief surrounded by snakes, with few incised details to mark facial features and limbs assuming the form of stems and tubes.

OTHER ELEMENTS

Some other elements, besides classical and folk or tribal type were also discerned. In this context, in the wood-carvings of Jaunsar-Bawar and Rawain region it was interesting to note in a panel at Kuna, the costume of a warrior chief and some reclining figures above shown lying in the background (probably the dead bodies). The costume of the male figures and seemingly dead figures in the background suggests the depiction of a battle ground. Though most of the carvings on the pillars at Kuna are related to the episodes from *Mahabharata*, this panel could be representation of the battle based on some folklore narrating some battle of the local chiefs (heroes) with alien forces. My thesis is based on the various historical records which mention the frequent fights between the local chiefs for expansion of their fiefdoms. The round type of the turban with diagonal rows of tiny squares, a long sleeve-less V-shaped coat fastened at the waist, apparently indicates the local attire. It is heavily decorated with zig-zag vertical pattern giving impression of an armour. The twelve-armed goddess Durga is also shown somewhat in similar attire which is sufficient to suggest that the carver Boda Badi conceived the gods and goddesses also in the costume of a warrior since *devi* was engaged in a battle, against the *rakshasas*.

The presumption of doning an armour doesnot sound logical since similar design on the dress is also noticed on the dress of the priest engaged in performing *aarti* with a lamp (*deep* or *diya*) and bell (*ghanti*).

A typical alien impact was noticed in the old temple of Pawasi *devata* at Chinwa, which has now been demolished. The lost wooden panel depicted two female revelers holding each others handa and dancing with a *dhapali*-like instrument held in their other hands. It bears close resemblance to the 'Dancing Duet' of Mughal school, dated 1700 A.D. in Bharat Kala Bhawan, Varanasi. Besides, some warriors astride horses are carved with modern guns though not directly related to Brahminical sources, but these features are noteworthy to comprehend how external elements were creeping into the art of wood carvings in this region either through their surroundings or the historic events passed on from generation to generation through folklore and legends. Use of punch marks to decorate figures was also a typical features of the wooden panels of the old (now demolished) temple at Chinwa and other centres. A possibility of the alien element has to be probed in the politico- historical background of this region. There are historical reference to prove that there have been interactions between the Mughals and the natives.

The Garhwal ruler Balbhadra Pal (A.D. 1581-1590) who once tried to revolt against Akbar but ultimately established good relations with the emperor, in the latter's fashion adopted the surname '*Shah*' (king — symbolic of sovereignty) in place of 'Pal' and came to be known as Balbhadra Shah. The tradition continues to be followed by the descendants of the royal house of Tehri (Garhwal) even today.[2]

"Mughal forces under *faujdar* Nijabat Khan supported by Sirmaur and Kumaon rajas were successful in annexing the Doon Valley from Garhwal but met disaster in the attempt to advance deeper into the hills. Though normalcy in their relation with the Mughals was restored, an incident later created tension between the two. During the struggle for succession of the royal throne among the Mughal princes Aurangzeb and Dara, Suleman Shikoh the latter's son who was on the run for his life, was granted asylum in Garhwal by its ruler in A.D. 1658."[2] But history bears testimony to the fact that such interactions also left-their imprints on the art of the period and place. Sikh *guru* designate Ram Rai came and settled in the quiet solitude of Doon Valley of Gawrhal. "He was a lover of art as we can infer from a number of miniature paintings (mainly of the Sikh *gurus* and his kin) which he got executed for this personnel collection. Some of them are still in the custody of the Mahant. They are believed to have been painted for him by some Mughal artists in c. 1685[30] who probably accompanied him to Dehradun.[31] Incidently the famous painting of Garhwal school brought to light by Mukandi Lal also owe their inception to the two painters of Mughal School — Shamdas and Kehar Das, who came here with prince Suleman when the latter sought shelter from the Garhwal ruler. Though the Mughal prince was later handed over to the imperial troops, both the artists were retained here. Mola Ram, credited with the inception of Garhwal school was their descendent."[4] Interaction between the immigrant and local artisans must have been a connatural phenomenon. Besides, the local artisans of hills must have occasionally visited the plains, thus giving them an opportunity for exposure to artistics activities in the nearby centres of paintings like Dehra Dun, Kankhal, Sirmaur and other hill states and Saharanpur — the hub of wood based art activities. Possibility of external impact in the local wood-carving of the hills cannot be ruled out.

In the wood carvings of the now demolished wooden temple at Chinwa, some males were noticed wearing long garment reaching ankles and decorated with beads and ribbon-like motifs. They also don a low cap with a pinnacle on it as seen on the right balcony or a very long cap as seen in the figure of a warrior on the railing of the rear balcony. A deity with swords in hands on the same railing wears a conical *chhatr*-type crown. Sometimes a turban type or an ornate crown also adorned their heads. The deep engraved folds on the skirts give them the appearance of heavily pleated lower garment reaching their ankles. The long cap-like crown on the heads of some of the male figures is also not a local element. Such features indicate the possibility of the influence of external factors as a result of socio-cultural interaction in the past.

A thorough study of the wood carvings in the region of Jaunsar-Bawar and Rawain clearly reveals creeping of modern elements and impact of the calendar art also. The gods and goddesses carved on the façade of the Mahasu *devata* temple at Zadi and the pediment under the gable roof of the verandah of the Mahasu *devata* temple at Hanol reveal strong impart of calendar art. Besides, modern element is also observed in another carving wherein two hands are shown with a *diya* (earthen lamp) in hands at Hanol (Pl.28). In this context it is noteworthy to observe the image of Mary Magdalene carved on one of the panels of a door of the temple of Chalda Mahasu at Lakhwar along with other Brahamanical deities carved on the rest of the panels. Besides, interestingly I also noticed on the arched door frame the image of Sai Baba carved on it. The architectural design of the present temple at Lakhwar has the impact of Buddhist pagoda type architecture on it. The old temple, now demolished, at Lakhwar had some carvings done on the wooden panels of the central verandah on four sides but we don't have any evidence left except its photographs.

Reference

1. Parthasarthy, *Op.Cit.*, P. 27.
2. Kamboj, B.P. *Early Wall Painting of Garhwal* ((Indus Publishing Company, New Delhi) p.21
3. *Ibid.*
4. *Ibid*, p. 25.

6

Conclusion

The socio-religio and religio-cultural panorama of Garhwal Himalaya is very rich. This region has dense forest area, which has been a source for the supply of wood as the primary raw material for construction of the religious and residential edifices, more specifically. Deodar, having insecticidal quality, increases its longevity. This quality, examined over the ages, is responsible for Deodar being considered as divine wood and hence, essentially used as the primary material by the natives in the construction of traditional temples – the abode of their gods. We find references about the instructions on the use of wood in architecture as early as the 6th and 7th cent. A.D.in our ancient texts like- *Vishnudharamottara* and the *Brihad Samhita* of Varah Mihir respectively. Besides, easy availability of the wood in the hilly regions of Garhwal Himalaya and due to heavy rainfall and snow fall observed in the region, wood has served as the congenial building material. Naturally, it provided great scope for the growth of art of carving in the Himalayan region as well as the indigenous techno- aspects associated with it, over the centuries in the past. The Khasas have played a significant role in the development of wooden architecture of the region, as they are known for their skill as wood-carvers.

The outstanding centres of wood carvings in Garhwal Himalaya are Jaunsar-Bawar and Rawain. Exquisite examples of wood carving in Jaunsar-Bawar are located at Hanol, Lakhwar, Lakhamandal, Zadi, and Kuna. The main centres of wood carvings in Rawain region are Thadiyar, Kharsali, Sankari, Pujaili, Naitwar, Than, Saur, Arakot, Koti-Kanesar, Chinwa, Devalsari and Deorah.

The most venerated deity of these two regions is Mahasu *devata*. Majority of the temples of the area are dedicated to this deity, The cult of Mahasu *devata* reached this region of Uttarakhand from Kashmir and is a non Brahmanical cult. Vedic Brahmanism of the Vedic period is considered to be historical predecessor of Hinduism. Pauranic Hinduism is the further evolution of the form. Prior to the advent of Mahasu cult in the regions of our study, the most venerated deities of here had been Shiv, *Devi, Surya* and Ganesh. There are 5,000 years old written records which reveal that the entire Uttarakhand was a stronghold of Vedic culture. Shavism in the region received a setback due to growing influence of Buddhism. Revival of Brahamnical religion in this region owes its debt to the visit of Shankracharya who injected a new soul into the erstwhile lost glory of Brahmanical cult. The latter lost its popularity among the indigenous people after the advent of Mahasu cult from Kashmir in the present area of study. According to a local belief Mahasu brothers, i.e. Botha, Basik, Pawasi and Chalda, defeated Vishnu in a battle and was given a secondary place. Consequently the Brahmanical gods of the Nagar temples of the region of study were removed and face-images of Mahasu *devata* and his pantheology were installed in the temple-cella. The temple of Mahasu *devata* at Hanol bears testimony to this fact.

So far as religious architecture is concerned, prolific depiction of the Brahamnical themes taken from *Ramayan, Mahabharat* and Pauranic sources as well as the Hindu gods and goddesses and Brahmanical symbols and motifs are found even at a prolusory examination of the carvings on the wooden architectural components. At times, we also come across very exquisitely carved designs and motifs which often adorn the exterior of the edifices.

The Brahmanical cult in the hilly regions of Jaunsar-Bawar and Rawain of Uttarakhand, though might have got influenced by the growing popularity of Mahasu cult and the local gods and goddesses, yet thematic depiction of episodes drawn from *Mahabharat, Ramayan, Purans* etc., on the exterior of the religious wooden buildings of the region bear testimony to the fact that venerability of the Brahmanical gods, goddesses and popular characters and heroes from the literary Brahmanical texts did not vanish. It enjoyed consistent existence along with the more popular cult of Mahasus and other local deities in the life and ethos of the natives.

The wood carvings of Jaunsar-Bawar and Rawain regions are marked by quintessential, sonorous craftsmanship. Gangaram is a living legendary veteran craftsman of the region who had been engaged in the construction and reconstruction work of the religious architecture. The exquisite craftsmanship of the temple of Basic *devata* at Kuna is credited to Bona Badi, who was blessed with divine skills of great expertise in art of wood carvings, as has been revealed by extraordinary specimens of his craftsmanship. Some other artisans engaged in the renovation of the temples in the region belonged to three patties of Uttarakhand, viz., (1) Chinwa, Gokul, Moda, Balauta, Kiratu; (ii) Mutanu, Maijani, Kiroli, Pauli, Makudi, 'Thurana, Baijgala, Kukreda; (iii) Masmorta, Saras, Bamlu, Thali, Devari.

Among the thematic depiction carved on the wooden components of edifices of this region, episodes taken from Raman had been quite popular. Often the trio of Lord Rama, Sita and Laxman is frequently carved. Other scenes from *Ramayan* include; Sita -*swayamvar*, Sita in Ashok-*vatika* Hanuman presenting Lord Ram's ring to Sita, Hanuman flying with mountain containing *sanjeevani*, Lanka-*dahan,* Crossing of the ocean, Lord Ram aiming with bow and arrow at the personification of the ocean to punish it, Lord Ram arming at the golden stag and Hanuman presenting Sita's *churamani* to Lord Ram etc.

Episodes taken from the epic *Mahabharat*, have also found profuse manifestation in the wood carvings of the religious architecture of this region, viz., Bhism lying on the bed of arrows, Arjun in disguise of Brihanala with prince Uttar of Viratnagar, Abhimanyu with the wheel of his chariot in hands in the battle field, *Cheer-haran*, Arjun aiming at the eye of the fish with his arrow with the help of its reflection in the water pond (a scene related to Draupadi's *swayamvar*), Dushashan dragging Draupadi, *Chakravyooh* and *Kamalvyooh* (army formations of defence on the battle field). It is interesting to note that live performance of *chakravyooh* is a part of the cultural performances in Alakhanda, Mandakini, Pindar and Bhagirathi valleys of Pindar. There is a temple dedicated to Duryodhan at Saur and Karn at Deoraha in the Rawain region. Besides, the festival in this region known as *Devlang parv* is held commemorating the struggle for superiority between the Kauravs and the Pandavs.

Genealogy of the gods and goddesses of Pauranic origin, life and deeds of gods like Krishn Shiv and Vishnu have been popular subject matter of wood-carving in the region. Krishn-*leela*, miraculous events from his life, e.g., like Krishn holding elephant *Kuvalyapeed, Kalia- Mardan, Rasa-leela, Vastra-haran,* , Shishupal-vadh, Krishn playing flute or Putana-*vadh*, Krishn crushing Trinavarta etc have found frequent manifestation in wood carvings. Among the various individual figures of gods and goddesses carved are Hanuman, Ram, Shiv, Vishnu, Kartikey. Laxmi, Saraswati, Mahisasurmardani, Nava-Durgas, eighteen-armed goddess Durga, Vishnu in Varahavatar, Ganesh, Brahma etc.

Essentially the symbolic nature of Indian art is also well reflected in the wood carvings of the religious architecture of Jaunsar-Bawar and Rawain regions also noticed on the wooden components of the secular architecture. Most commonly used symbols in carvings are sun-motif, *swastik, puranghat, trishul*, fish, snakes – single or double or inter-twined or *Nagraj* and *Navagrahs.* Besides scrolls, stylized floral or geometrical decorative motifs are also noticed.

A thorough study of the wood carvings of Garhwal Himalaya reveals splendid scenario and ethos of enchanting, rich, sonorous religious- cultural heritage of the natives of this region. The indigenous artisans have produced very original art work and shown their innovative skills in finding their own solutions to the problem of the space limitation of the wooden panels. Sometimes, a complex scene or episode continues from one panel to another . It is remarkable to note the use of platform-like form to raise the height of the figure, e.g., in the episode wherein Lord Ram aims at the golden stag, the latter is placed on a platform to bring him to the level of the arrow.

The wood work of the region reveals classical strains as well as folk and tribal impact. Classical strains are particularly noticeable in the carvings of Pauranic gods and goddesses at Hanol, Kuna, Lakhwar, Than, Pujaili etc. These strains can be witnessed in the depiction of classical deities with traditional iconographical details. Sometimes their depiction gets complex as can be seen in the image of eighteen-armed goddess *Devi* at Hanol, or the *tribhang* posture of figures.

It is difficult to believe that the classical elements could have come down to the wood-carvers traditionally. However, easy access to the modern prints and calendars of the gods and goddesses available in the market, is bound to have its impact on the native art. It is for this reason that we often notice the presence of folk, tribal and classical strains simultaneously. As discussed earlier it was noticed at Zaidi, Kuna, Sankri, Koti-Kanesar, Thadiyar, Hanol etc. The folk element is visible in the treatment of figures and forms in a given space of a wooden panel or component, and with scant concern for realism, depth, perspective, anatomy etc. The carvers have treated the limbs of figures like tube or flexible stem of a plant, and their body could be given any desirable twist or turn, as per availability of space restricted by the fixed limits of the panels or wooden components as, e.g., can be seen. Durgas image on the panel of the wooden column at Kuna. But, on the other hand, the palanquin bears at Kuna as shown in tribal type constume, often depicted in very lively walking movement.

The independent wooden image of Bhairav at Sankari is having strong folk impact. Another similar image was noticed lying in the grilled verandah at Hanol under the custody of Archaeological Survey of India. Besides, in wooden temples there had been a practice of placing independent image of a goat or munal on the *kurad* of the temple. Goat heads in high relief sometimes project from architectural components, as at Sankari, Naitwar and Saur. Goats are sacrificed in the temples and considered auspicious. Wooden image of snarling leopard seen at many places, very folkish in appearance, are generally placed at the sides of the entrance door, like at noticed at

Rudreshwar Mahadev temple at Devalsari and Bhairav temple Sankari.

Besides many other element also characterize these wood carvings. They reveal the impact of the calendar art. Depiction of some popular non-Brahmanical personalities like Sai Baba and popular modern motifs like depiction of a *diya* (earthen lamp) placed on the two hands, so commonly seen on Diwali greeting cards. Still more interesting to note is the Depiction of Mary Magdalene on one of the penals of a door of the temple of Chalda Mahasu alongwith other Brahmanical deities at Lakhwar.

Due to perishable quality of the wood, wooden edifices have been periodically renovated or at times, even replaced entirely with a new structure, as was found by the author at the temple of Pawasi *devata* at Chinwa. Due to the ignorance of the locals, the precious, antique carved wooden panels have been lost forever, except a couple of panels found lying at the site fortunately. The site was also visited earlier by the author in 2002 and its full documentation done. The same has also been discussed along with the new wooden carvings in Chapter IV of the book.

The glimpses of wood carving of Garhwal Himalaya forming part of the architectural components of wooden edifies reveals that it projects a magnificent panorama of themes derived from varied religious sources. At times, amalgamation of subject matter of contemporary relevance also finds manifestation. Remarkable to note is the local artisans innovative methods and mannerism to resolve the problems posed by space division and restriction of space available as per the framework of the architectural components. These also bear testimony to socio-religious upheavals occurring in the region, resulting in dominance of one faith or belief over the other and increasing popularity of local faiths and cults over the Brahamanical cults which was the main factor in depicting the subject matter related to the latter at the exterior of the temples located in the region, whereas, the temple sanctum enshrins the face images and idols of the local gods and goddess venerated in the centres already discussed in the book. The renovation of these wooden edifies is often carried out without any concern and awareness of the cultural and aesthetic significance they possess at the national and international level. Besides, wood being costly material, this is being replaced by stone and concrete. Consequently, timely relevant steps and measured need to be taken by ASI and the government and non-government organization to conserve the cultural heritage of Garhwal Himalaya which possesses a rich repertoire of the religio-cultural and socio-cultural heritage of the hills.

Bibliography

Primary Sources

Mahabharata, (tr.) Paramhans Swami Jagdishwar Nand Saraswati, Part I, (Govindram Hansanand, Delhi, 1983).

Rigveda, (Dayanand Sansthan, New Delhi).

Srimadvalmikiya Ramayan, Part I, (Geeta Press, Gorakhpur).

Secondary Sources

Agarwal, O.P. 'A study of Indian Polychrome Wooden Sculpture' in, *Studies in Conservation*, vol., No.2 (May, 1971).

Arts of the Earth; Folk and Tribal Art of India, (Art & Deal, New Delhi, 2010).

Atkinson, E.T., *The Himalayan Gazetteer*, Vol. I, Part I (Cosmo Publication, Delhi, 1973).

Atkinson, E.T., The Himalayan Gazetteer, Vol. II, Part I (Cosmo Publication, Delhi, 1973).

Atkinson, E.T., *The Himalayan Gazetteer*, Vol. II, Part II (Cosmo Publication, Delhi, 1973).

Atkinson, E.T., *The Himalayan Gazetteer*, Vol. III, Part I (Cosmo Publication, Delhi, 1973).

Bangroo, Virendra, 'Indigenous Architectural Heritage of Kashmir' in, *Heritage of Jammu, Kashmir and Ladakh*, ed. by Badam, G.L., & Chakravorty, K.K. (Research India Press, 2010).

Baumer, Bettwa (Ed.) *Rupa-Pratirupa* (Biblia Impex Pvt. Ltd., New Delhi, 1982).

Bhaktivedanta, A.C., *The Supreme Personality of Godhead* (Bhaktivedanta Book Trust, Calif).

Bhatt, G.S., *Women and polyandry in Rawain Jaunpur* (Rawat Publications, New Delhi, 1991).

Brown, Percy, *Indian Architecture*, (Bombay, 1949).

Buhlar, G.,"The Prasasti of the Temple of Lakhamandal," in *Epigraphia Indica*, Vol. I (1982).

Coomarswamy, A.K., *Transformation of Nature in Art* (Munishram, Manoharlal Publishers Pvt. Ltd, New Delhi, 1974).

Dabral, Shivaprasad, *Uttarakhand Ka Itihas*, Part III (Hindi) (Virgatha Prakashn, Dugada, Garhwal).

Danosi, B.L., *Garhwal Ke Shilpakaro Ka Itihas*, (Hindi) (Vinsar Publishing Company, Dehradun, 2006).

Duran, Jane, 'The Nagaraja, Symbol and Symbolism in Hindu Art and Iconography', in *Journal of Aesthetic Education*, Vol. 24, No.2 (Sumer, 199).

Emigh, John, 'Dealing with the Demonic, : Strategies for Containment in Hindu Iconography and Performance', in *Asian Theatre Journal*, no.1 (University of Hawaii Press, Spring 1984).

Encyclopaedia Britanica, (A society of Gentlemen, Scotland, 1968).

Garhwal Himalaya; Nature, Culture & Society, Editors-Kandari, O.P. & Gusain, O.P. (Trans Media, Media House, Srinagar, Garhwal, 2001).

Gulia, K.S., Art and Culture of Himalayas, (Isha Books, New Delhi, 2007).

Ghosh, S.P., Hindu Religious Art and Architecture, (D.K. Publications, Delhi, 1982).

Guitrand, Felix (Ed.), *The New Larousee Encylopedia of Mythology* (Tr.), (Hamlyn Publishing Group Ltd., U.S.A., 1968).

Gupta, Parmeshwarilal, Bhartiya Vastukala (Hindi), (Vishwavidyalaya Prakashan, Varanasi, 1981).

Handa,Om Chand, *Pahari Folk Art* (D.BN. Taraporevala Sons & Co., Bombay, 1975).

Handa, Om Chand, *Pashchmi Himalaya Ki Lok Kalayen* (Hindi) (Indus Publishing Company, New Delhi, 1988).

Handa, O.C., 'An Archaeological Case Study of a temple in Jaunsar-Bawar Area in Uttar Pradesh' (A Seminar Paper presented at Indian Institute of Advanced Study, Rastrapati Niwas, Shimla, 1996).

Handa, O.C. *Temple Architecture of Western Himalayas: Wooden Temple* (Indus Publishing Company, New Delhi, 2001).

Handa, O.C. *History of Uttaranchal* (Indus Publishing Company, New Delhi, 2002)

Handa, O.C. *Naga Cults and Traditions in the Western Himalayas* (Indus Publishing Company, New Delhi, 2004).

Handa, O.C. *Himalayan Traditional Architecture* (Rupa Company New Delhi, 2009).

Handa, O.C. *Naga Wood Carvings in the Himalayan Region* (Indus Publishing Company, New Delhi, 2006).

Handa, O.C. & Jain, Madhu, *Wood Handicrafts, A Study of Its Origin and Development in Saharanpur* (Indus Publishing Company, New Delhi, 2000).

Harimohan, *Hamara Uttaranchal* (Hindi) (Hindi Book Centre, New Delhi, 2002).

Havell, E.B. *Indian Architecture Through the Ages* (Asian Publication Services, India, 1978).

Ions, Veronica, *Indian Mythology* (Bounty Books, London, 2004).

Jain, Madhu, *The abode of Mahashiva; Cults and Symbology in Jaunsar-Bawar in Mid-Himalaya* (Indus Publishing Company, New Delhi, 1995).

Joshi, P. *Glimpses of Hindu Cults and Culture* (Sundeep Prakash, Delhi, 1997).

Joshi, N.P. *Bhartiya Murti-Vigyan* (Hindi) (Bihar Rastra Bhasha Parishad, Patna).

Kamboj, B.P. *Early Wall Painting of Garhwal* (Indus Publishing Company, New Delhi, 2003).

Kamboj, Richa, *Wooden Temples of Uttarakhand A study of Art & Architecture* (Indus Publishing Company, New Delhi, 2010).

Kaur, Jagdish, *Himalaya : Pilgrimages and New Tourism* (Himalayan Books, New Delhi, 1985).

Kramrisch, Stella, *The Hindu Temples*, Vol. I, (University of Calcutta, 1976).

Kramrisch, Stella, *Indian Sculptures* (Motilal Banarasidas, Delhi, 1981).

Lal, Prem Hari Har, *Doon Valley Down the Ages* (Inter Prints, New Delhi, 1993).

Lommel, Andreas, *Prehistoric and Premitive Man* (Paul Himlyn, 1966).

Madhavacharya & Digvijaybai, Shankracharya Vijai.

Madhya Himalaya ki Anusuchita Evam Pichadi Jatiya, Parampara, Shilpa aur Vidhan, ed., M.P. Joshi, (Almora Book Depot, Almora, 2011).

Mathapal, *Yashodhara, Uttarakhand Ka Kasthashilpa* (Bishansingh Mahendrapal, Dehradun, 1997).

Majumdar, D.N. *Races & Cultures of India* (Universal Publishers Ltd., Lucknow, 1944).

Maxwell, T.S. 'Lakhamandal and Trilokinath,' an *Art International*, Vol. XXIV /1-2 (Sept.- Oct. 1980).

Mishra, Ramanath, Bhartiya Murtikala (Hindi), (Macmillan Company of India Limited, New Delhi, 1978).

Mitchell, A.G. *Hindu Gods and Goddesses* (Nutech Photo Lithographers, Delhi, 2001).

Mitra, Rathin, *Temples of Garhwal and other Landmarks* (Garhwal Mandal Vikas Nigam, Delhi, 1994).

Mohta, Surajmal, *Bhagwat Katha* (Hindi) (Sasta Sahitya Mandal Prakashan, New Delhi, 1994).

Mukherjee, Radhakamal, *Social Function of Art* (Hindi Kitab Ltd., Bombay, 1951).

Mukherjee, Radhakamal, The Culture and Art of India, (George Allen & Unwin Ltd., London, 1959).

Nagar, S.L. *Siva in Art, Literature and Thought* (Indus Publishing Company, New Delhi, 1994).

Naithani, Shivaprasad, *Uttaranchal Ke Tirth Aivam Mandir* (Hindi) (Parvatiya Prakashan, Srinagar, Garhwal, 1997).

Natuiayl Shivananda, *Kedar Badri Yatra Darshan* (Hindi) (Sulabh Prakashan, Lucknow, 1988).

Nautiyal, Shivananda, *Garhwal Ka Sanskritik Vaibhav* (Hindi) (Uttar Madhya Sanskritik Kendra, Allahabad, 1994).

Negi, S.S. 'Back and the Beyond' in *Garhrwal Himalaya, Nature Culture & Society* (Ed.) O.P. Gusain, O.P. Kandari, (Trans Media, Srinagar, Garhwal).

Pandey, B.D. *Lok Kala Evam Shilpa – Kumayun* (Hindi) (State Lalit Kala Akademi, U.P., 1998).

Pant, Pushpesh & Dilwali, Ashok, *The Garhwal Himalayas: Ramparts of Heaven* (Lustre Press Pvt. Ltd., 1987).

Parrish, Y.M., Cross Land, Y.R., & Harland, A.W. (Ed.), *The New Standard Encyclopedia and World Atlas* (The Times of India, Bombay, 1936).

Parthasarthy, V.R. & Parthasarthy, Indu, *Devi Goddesses in Indian Art and Literature* (Bharatiya Kal Prakashan, Delhi, 2009).

Pattanaik, V. *Vishnu : An Introduction* (Vakils, Feffer and Simons Ltd., Mumbai, 2000).

Rajan, K.V.S. *India's Religious Art* (Cosmo Publication, New Delhi, 1982).

Rawat, Ajay Singh, *Garhwal Himalayas; A Historical Survey* (1815-1947) (Eastern Book Linkem, Delhi, 1983).

Rawat, Ajay S. *Garhwal Himalaya : A Study in Historical Perspective* (Indus Publishing Company, New Delhi).

Saili Ganesh, *The Doon Valley Across the Years* (Rupa Co., New Delhi, 2007).

Sahni, Rai Bahadur Daya Ram, *'Lakhamandal'*, in Annual Report of Archaeological Survey of India, 1923-24, S.J. Marshall (Ed.).

Sharma, D.D. *Cultural History & Uttaranchal* (Indira Gandhi National Centre for Arts, New Delhi).

Sharma, D.D. *Uttarakhand Ke Lok_Devata* (Hindi) (Ankit Publishers, Haldwani, 2006).

Shukla, D.N. *Vastu-Sastra*, Vol. II, (Munshiram Manoharlal Publishers Pvt. Ltd., 1993).

Singh, Bhajan, *Aryon Ka Adi Niwas, Madhya Himalaya*, (Hindi) (Bhagirathi Prakashan, Tehri, 1980).

Singh, Girish Chandra, *Puratatvik Sarvekshan Report, 1984-85-86* (Hindi), (Kshetriya Puratatva Ikai, Pauri Garhwal, 1993).

Singh, Sushil Kumar, *Cultural History of Northern India* (Ramananda Vidya Bhawan, New Delhi, 1986).

Smith, H.D., & M.Narasimha, *Handbook of Hindu Gods, Goddesses and Saints* (Sundeep Prakashan, Delhi, 1991).

Srvastava, Rakesh Kumar, *Pindar Ghati Ki Puratatvik Sarvekshan Report, 1987-88* (Hindi) (Kshetriya Puratatva Ikai, Garhwal, 1988).

Stein, Jess (Ed.), *The Random House Dictionary* (Allied Publishers Pvt. Ltd., Bombay, 1972).

Tewari, S.P.*Hindu Iconography* (Agam Kala Prakashan, New Delhi, 1979).

Thakur, L.S. *Where Mortals and Mountain Gods Meet; Society and Culture in Himachal Pradesh* (Indian Institute of Advanced Study, Rashtrapatinivas, Shimla, 2002).

Sairam, T.V. *Indian Temples; Forms and Foundations* (Agam Kala Prakashan, Delhi, 1982).

Saklani, D.P. *Ramayan Tradition in Historical Perspective* (Ruchika Printers, Delhi, 2006).

Saklani, Pradeep & Nautiyal, Vinod, 'Archaeology: A New Perspective' in, *Garhwal Hiamalaya: Nature, Culture & Society* (Trans Media, Srinagar, Garhwal).

Saraswati, B.N., Mallik, S.C., Khanna, Madhu (Ed.), *Art the Integral Vision* (D.K. Print World, New Delhi, 1994).

Sati, S.P., & Sati, M.C. *Uttarakhand Statehood : Dimensions of Development* (Indus Publishing Company, New Delhi, 2000).

Thapar, Romila, *A History of India*, Vol. I, (Penguin Books, 1990).

Tiwari, Rakesh, *Sarvekshan Report, 1981-82-83* (Hindi) (Parvatiya Puratatva Ikai, Almora, 1984).

Tomery, E. *Introduction to the History of Fine Art in India and the West* (Orient Longman Ltd., New Delhi, 1968).

Vaidyanathan, Sunil, *Ganesha–The God of India* (English Edition Publishers and Distributors (I) Pvt. Ltd., Mumbai, 2003).

Venkateshwara, S.V., 'The Development of Early Hindu Iconography,' in, *Journal of the Royal Asiatic Society of Great Britain and Ireland* (Jul 1917).

Verma, Paripurna Nanda, *Prateek Shastra* (Hindi), (Hindi Samiti, Information Deptt. U.P., 1964).

Uttaranchal A Cultural Kaleidoscope (Uttaranchal Tourism Development Board, India, 2004).

Walton, H.G. *British Garhwal : A Gazetteer* (Government Press, Allahabad, 1910).

Walton, H.G. *Gazetteer of British Garhwal* (Natraj Publishers, Dehradun, 1989).

Walton, H.G. *Gazetteer of Dehradun* (Natraj Publishers, Dehradun, 1995).

Williams, G.R.C. *Memoir of Dehradun* (Natraj Publishers, Dehradun, 1998).

Plates

Plate 1: Temple of Mahasu devata, Hanol

Plate 2: The door of the Sabha-Mandap, Mahasu Temple, Hanol.

Plate 3: Detail of the door of the Sabha-Mandap, Mahasu Temple, Hanol.

Plate 4: Detail of the door of the Sabha-Mandap, Mahasu Temple, Hanol.

Plate 5: Detail of the door of the Sabha-Mandap, Mahasu Temple, Hanol.

Plate 6: Navgraha *Symbols, Ceiling of the Porch, Mahasu Temple, Hanol*

Plate 7: Pediment of the Porch, Mahasu Temple, Hanol.

Plate 8: Panel under the roof (right side), Mahasu Temple, Hanol.

Plate 9: Bhairav, Mahasu Temple, Hanol.

Plate 10: Pillar (detail), Shiv Temple, Lakhamandal.

Plate 11: Entrance door of the temple-verandah, Basik devata Temple, Kuna.

Plate 12: Door of the temple cella, Basik devata Temple, Kuna.

Plate 13: Detail of the cella-wall (exterior), Basik devata Temple, Kuna.

Plate 14: Wooden pillar in the verandah, Basik devata temple, Kuna.

Plate 15: Wooden pillar in the verandah, Basik devata Temple, Kuna.

Plate 16: Detail of a panel, Basik devata Temple, Kuna.

Plate 17: Detail of a panel, Basik devata Temple, Kuna.

Plate 18: Residential building on way to Karn Temple, Deorah

Plate 19: Temple of Mahasu devata, Lakhwar.

Plate 20: Old Temple of Mahasu devata, Lakhwar.

Plate 21: Entrance door, Assembly Hall, Mahasu Temple, Lakhwar.

Plate 22: Entrance Door, Temple of Chalda Mahasu, Lakhwar.

Plate 23: Entrance, Assembly Hall (detail), Mahasu Temple, Lakhwar.

Plate 24: Pillar of a residential building, Lakhwar.

Plate 25: Wood work on an architectural component of a residential building, Lakhwar.

Plate 26: Detail of an arched door-frame, temple of Chalda Mahasu, Thadiyar.

Plate 27: Detail of arched door-frame, temple of Chalda Mahasu, Thadiyar.

Plate 28: Wooden column, verandah, temple of Jamdagni Rishi, Than.

Plate 29: Wooden column, verandah, temple of Jamdagni Rishi, Than.

Plate 30: Detail of the wooden wall of mandap (exterior), Composite - Roofed Someshwar Temple, Kharsali.

Plate 31: Ventilator, Composite-Roofed Someshwar Temple, Kharsali.

Plate 32: Temple of Bhairav, Sankari.

Plate 33: Wooden Sculpture of Bhairav, Sankari

Plate 34: Wooden Beam (detail), Bhairav Temple, Sankari.

Plate 35: Wooden Column, Bhairav Temple, Sankari.

Plate 36: Wooden Lion Sculpture, Bhairav Temple, Sankari.

Plate 37: Door Jambs, Raghunath Temple, Pujali.

Plate 38: Door Jambs, Raghunath Temple, Pujali.

Plate 39: Secular edifice, Raghunath Temple, Pujaili.

Plate 40: Wooden panel (detail) with face image, cella, Duryodhan Temple, Saur.

Plate 41: Details of the Façade, Duryodhan Temple, Saur.

Plate 42: Goat and Munal images placed on the Kurad, Duryodhan Temple, Saur.

Plate 43: Entrance door, Temple of Kaun devata, Arakot.

Plate 44: Temple of Pawasi devata (now Demolished), Chinwa.

Plate 45: Panels of now demolished Temple of Pawasi devata, Chinwa.

Plate 46: Panels of now demolished Temple of Pawasi devata, Chinwa.

Plate 47: Temple of Pawasi devata, Chinwa.

Plate 48: Entrance door, Temple of Pawasi devata, Chinwa.

Plate 49: Navgrah symbols (ceiling), Temple of Pawasi devata, Chinwa.

Plate 50: Veteran Craftsman, Gangaram.

Plate 51: Façade (detail), Temple of Mahasu devata, Zaidi.

Plate 52: Temple of Karn, Deorah.

Plate 53: Ceiling (detail), Temple of Karn, Deorah.

Plate 54: Rudreshwar Mahadev Temple, Devalsari.

Plate 55: Verandah, Rudreshwar Mahadev Temple, Devalsari.

Plate 56: Temple of Kali, Koti-Kanesar.

Plate 57: Entrance Door, Temple of Kali, Koti-Kanesar.

Plate 58: Detail of panel, Pokhu devta temple, Naitwar.

Plate 59: Temple of Mahasu devata, Kurwa.

Plate 60: Entrance door, Temple of Mahasu devata, Kurwa.

Plate 61: Residences, Lakhwar.

Plate 62: Entrance door of a house, Lakhwar.

Plate 63: The author with local ladies, Lakhwar.

Plate 64: Detail of a column in the verandah of a house, Lakhwar.

Plate 65: A wooden plank supporting the roof of a house, Lakhwar.

Plate 66: Verandah of a house, Lakhwar.

Plate 67: Interior of a wooden house and a hukkha with wooden parts.

Plate 68: A wooden niche type component for collecting honey, Lakhwra

Plate 69: Wooden Churn- staff holder, Lakhwar.

Plate 70: Wooden hook, Lakhwar.

Plate 71: Wooden boxes, Lakhwar.

Plate 72: Residences at Dharali, Uttarkashi.

Plate 73: Detail of the wooden balcony of a house, Dharali, Uttarkashi.

Plate 74: Wooden balcony of a house, Lakhamandal.

Plate 75: Wooden railing of a house, Lakhamandal.

Plate 76: Wooden pillar of a house, Lakhamandal.

Plate 77: Detail of a wooden component of a house, Lakhamandal.

Plate 78: A residential architecture, Lakhamandal.

Plate 79: Exterior of a house Arkot.

Plate 80: Wooden verandah of a house, Arkot.

Plate 81: Detail of the pillar of a house, Arkot.

Plate 82: Wood work on the exterior of a house, Arkot.

Plate 83: Detail of the wooden railing of a house, Chakrata

Plate 84: Wooden door of an old haveli *(now demolished), Dehradun.*

Plate 85: Wooden door of a house, Dehra Dun.

Line Drawings

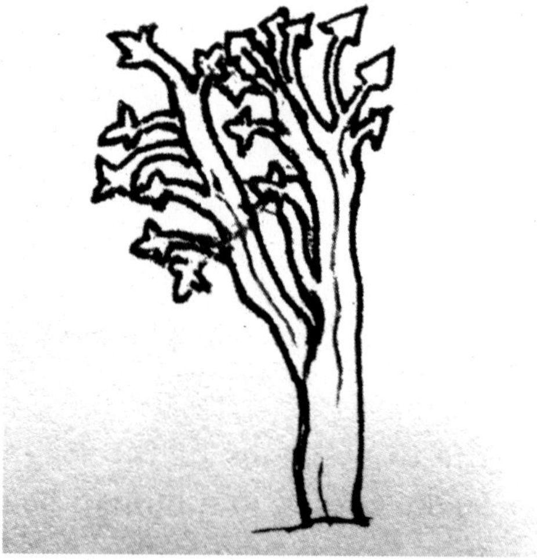

Line Drawing 1: Tree, Thadiyar

Line Drawing 2: Sun, Chinwa

Line Drawing 3: Mrinal, Chinwa

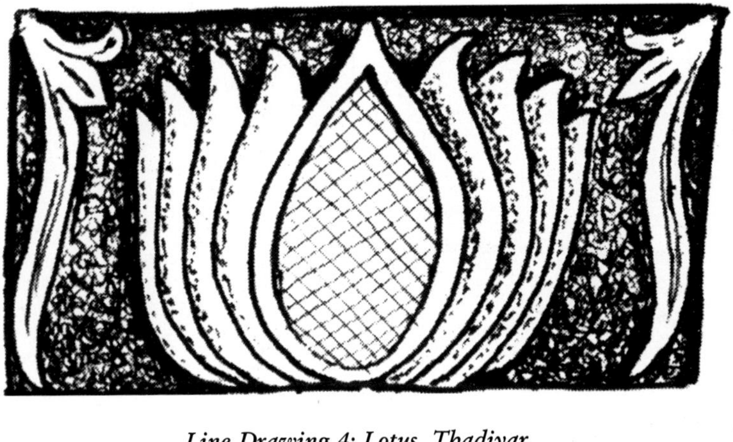

Line Drawing 4: Lotus, Thadiyar

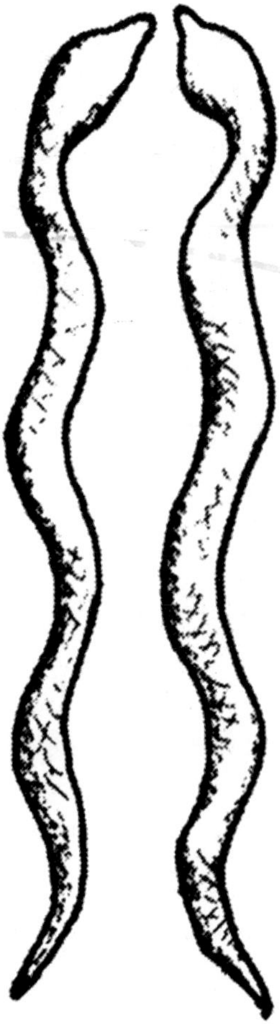

Line Drawing 5: A Pair of Snakes, Lakhamandal.

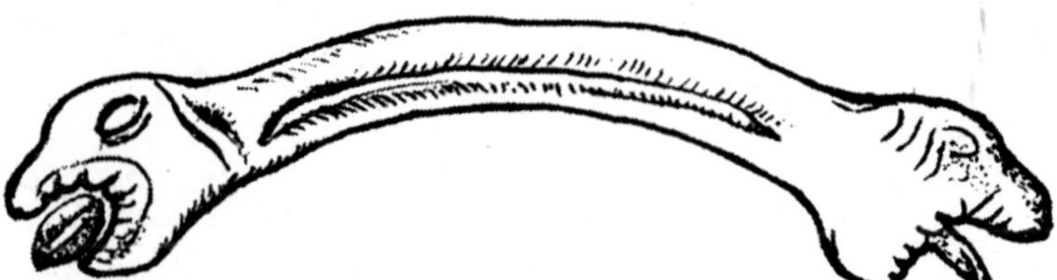

Line Drawing 6: A Motif with Lion Heads, Deorah

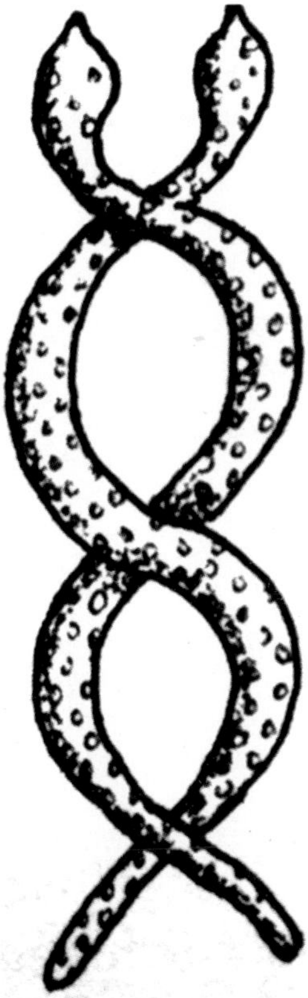

Line Drawing 7: Entwined snakes, Hanol.

Line Drawing 8: Wooden leopard in 3-D in the porch of Bhairav temple, Sankari

Line Drawing 9: Naga Devata, Chinwa.

Line Drawing 10: Demon cutting the Earth-tree (a legend), the wooden post of the temple, Chinwa.

Line Drawing 11: Mahishasuramardani (wooden jamb of the cella door of the temple, Kuna

Line Drawing 12: Design engraved on the wooden ceiling of the temple, Deorah.

Index